Best Places to Stay

44 EXTRAORDINARY HOTELS

Best Places to Stay

44 EXTRAORDINARY HOTELS

PHOTOGRAPHY **GRANT SHEEHAN** | TEXT **SHELLEY-MAREE CASSIDY**

FIREFLY BOOKS

Thanks to: Ulrike Baumann, Anjali Nihalchand, Sin Sokhorn, Tong Ton, Lamey Chang, Toby Anderson, Nick Box, Kebonye Segobanyara and Todd Motingwa of Sandibe M.T., Sage and James of Nxabega, David Hamilton, Jenn Jordan and Marty Hunt.
All photographs by Grant Sheehan except Faena interior photos on pages 20 and 22, supplied by Faena Hotel + Universe.

Extract from *Blue Shoes and Happiness* by Alexander McCall Smith reproduced by permission of Polygon (www.birlinn.co.uk)

A Firefly Book

Published by Firefly Books Ltd. 2007

First printing

Publisher Cataloging-in-Publication Data (U.S.)

Sheehan, Grant.
    Best places to stay : 44 extraordinary hotels / Grant Sheehan and Shelley-Maree Cassidy.
[304] p. : col. photos. ; cm.
Summary: Featuring hotels from around the globe. Destinations range between modern, traditional, large, small, simple and luxurious and are diverse in style and price.
ISBN-13: 978-1-55407-293-4 (pbk.)
ISBN-10: 1-55407-293-X (pbk.)
1. Hotels — Guidebooks. 2. Resorts – Guidebooks. I. Cassidy, Shelley-Maree.
II. Title.
910.46 dc22   TX907.S544   2007

Library and Archives Canada Cataloguing in Publication

Sheehan, Grant
    Best places to stay : 44 extraordinary hotels / Grant Sheehan & Shelley-Maree Cassidy.
ISBN-13: 978-1-55407-293-4
ISBN-10: 1-55407-293-X
    1. Hotels—Guidebooks. 2. Hotels—Pictorial works.
I. Cassidy, Shelley-Maree II. Title.
TX907.S454 2007   910.46   C2007-900629-9

Published in the United States by
Firefly Books (U.S.) Inc.
P.O. Box 1338, Ellicott Station
Buffalo, New York 14205

Published in Canada by
Firefly Books Ltd.
66 Leek Crescent
Richmond Hill, Ontario L4B 1H1

Original design concept by: typeface ltd, www.typeface.co.nz

Printed in China

Contents

Introduction

There are so many places to go and so many hotels to choose from that deciding where to stay is not easy.

The hotels in this book are chosen for their style and interest and for where they are, not how much they cost for a night. It is an eclectic mix, each quite different from the other, in a variety of destinations, spanning city life to wildlife and landscapes in between. The photographs illustrate the hotel and its setting; to know what it looks like is the next best thing to going there.

While a holiday away from the habitual is revitalizing, we are affected in some way by everywhere we travel, to a lesser and greater degree. Many places have the power to change our views, challenge our beliefs and add an edge of the unexpected. It might be a "soft adventure" compared to scaling Mount Everest or kayaking in Antarctica, but it can be thought-provoking, stimulating and even life-changing all the same.

Travel hopefully, arrive with a positive attitude and appreciate the differences; and most of all just enjoy being somewhere else.

Your travel life has the essence of a dream. It is something outside the normal, yet you are in it. It is peopled with characters you have never seen before and in all probability will never see again. **It brings occasional homesickness, and loneliness and pangs of longing ... But you are like the Vikings** or the master mariners of the Elizabethan age, who have gone into the world of adventure, and home is not home until you return.

Agatha Christie

The use of traveling is to regulate imagination by reality, **and instead of thinking how things may be**, to see them as they are.
Samuel Johnson

This book is essentially about homes away from home for the traveler, about places to stay – the accommodation and the destinations. Hotels have always played a major part in travel, whether the purpose is business or pleasure. Often scenes of great events, mystery, intrigue and romance are contained within their walls, as may be history, both individual and international. The hotels featured here all distinguish themselves as fascinating places to stay, although each is as disparate and distinct as its guests.

In the era of the 747 no journey is so long that it is still much of an adventure reaching your destination. Negotiating airports and fellow passengers are often the most arduous elements. A click of the mouse now brings instant virtual access to the world and its cultures; actually being there seems to matter less and less. So, does travel still serve to broaden the mind? The desire to see for oneself is unchecked. More and more people are traveling, and tourism is the leading global industry.

Even in this age of instant information transfer, traveling involves mundane processes – booking tickets, packing and labeling luggage, and obtaining travel documents. The journey itself may be a smooth, uncomplicated passage or one with frustrating delays, bad service, lost luggage and expensive transfers. It is with a sense of relief that the traveler arrives at their destination. You reach your hotel, and whether modest or grand, old or new, it will serve as your temporary home away from home.

Afterglow

Cavas Wine Lodge Mendoza, Argentina

"Ah, Mendoza … " A smile, gentle sigh of envy and a look of remembered pleasures was the response of people in Buenos Aires when they heard our next destination in Argentina: north to the heart of wine country.

One of the first sights on leaving the airport is a vineyard; its rows lead almost right up to the runway. The smell of fresh mountain air breezes across a lush part of what is actually a desert-like climate, a dry sunny place where rain is scarce, but wine is abundant. There are nearly half a million acres of vineyards in this high-altitude region; grapes, olive and fruit trees are all nourished by a network of irrigation channels dating far back to the first Indian farming.

El Oasis Norte, the northern oasis, is home to some of the oldest plots of the country's signature wine grape: malbec. Quality, quantity and tradition make Mendoza the heart of all things wine-related in Argentina. "*El Malbec a uno mantiene vivo*" – "Malbec keeps one alive" is a local vintner's popular assertion. Merlot, cabernet sauvignon, syrah, tempranillo; classic whites of chardonnay, sauvignon and chenin blanc, riesling and more also thrive here for varietal sustenance.

In one such plot, at the end of a long dusty drive into the vines, what seems to be a tiny village comes into view. Small curved houses, set among and rising above the vines, cluster around the main house of Cavas Wine Lodge in a smooth blend of classic Spanish and innovative adobe architecture.

Lodge terrace at night

Centered in acres of its own bonarda and cabernet sauvignon vines, the lodge looks out to a mountainous horizon. The snow-capped blue foothills of the Andes stand to the west, and stretching before them as far as the eye can see, are green, gold and russet-leaved vineyards. The wine cellar – *cava* – is the foundation, literally, of the lodge. Underground, and stacked with dozens of Argentina's best labels, it is the source of the well considered matches that complement the palate-pleasing cuisine served in the restaurant above. Color, bouquet and aftertaste can be assessed and discussed further in the library or out on the terrace.

At night, braziers light the walkways to the main house for dinner, and back again to your vineta; a name unique to Cavas, derived from a blend of *vin* and *villetta*, a fit appellation for a villa in the heart of a vineyard.

The spa

From outside a futuristic take on traditional South American adobe structures, the vineta inside is a very well appointed modern apartment, cool whites enlivened with fiery red. Each has the added bonus of secluded outdoor living: its own terraced plunge pool for warm days and upstairs to a sunset and star-viewing platform on the roof, where on crisp nights logs and vine-clippings burning in the fireplace will give warmth and the primal satisfaction of flame-watching.

Cavas has an intriguing and eclectic art collection, from antique manikins, wood vine sculptures, sleek abstract bronze figures like greyhounds, to colorful textiles sourced from all over Argentina. There is style but not attitude here, it is a relaxed environment, but deluxe all the same.

Total immersion in wine can be practiced here. You can drink it and also bathe in it; treat yourself to the ancient Roman ritual of vinotherapy in the serene Moorish spa. A crushed malbec scrub – a combination of grape seeds and essential oils flushed pink like rosé – leaves skin smooth as satin for several days. A bonarda bath is a deep soak in bubbling red wine extracts, or try a wine wrap cosseted in warm wine yeast and honey. Wine may not ever touch your lips but it can be good for your skin.

There is style but not attitude here, **it is a relaxed environment**, but deluxe all the same.

A vineta

A vineta bedroom

Sunrise view of vinetas

Spanish conquistadors planted the first grapevines in this New World when they arrived in 1554. Winegrowing is now Argentina's main agricultural industry. The output from more than a thousand wineries – bodegas – makes it the fifth largest wine producer in the world, and growth in its wine culture is vigorous.

Mendoza is the premier wine region; so many vineyards are within easy reach of Cavas. Reservations are required to visit most bodegas; one list gave their favorite bodegas from best for stargazing to best dining, best barrel tasting, best at sunset; there could also be one for most dramatic architecture. That would go to the Mayan pyramid inspired design of Bodega Catena Zapata, the showpiece of one of Argentina's great winemaking families. Aromatherapy of a special sort is offered here, a heady perfume of wine pervades the state-of-the-art building; the tour guide says the team doesn't notice it but that visitors inhale deeply on arrival. It was harvesting time, and at the cellar door, orange tarpaulins were heaped high with grapes, black and gleaming like coal. The tasting rooms acquaint wine-lovers with samples of the end result; the world-class smooth velvety malbecs being made here, as well as cabernet sauvignon and chardonnay blends.

This is good *terroir* for climbers other than vines. Its mountainous landscape attracts the adventurous and energetic, or you can drive from here over and through the Andes to Chile. On the way you will likely see Cerro Aconcagua, the highest mountain peak outside the Himalayas. The high altitude, good wine and food at Cavas make some light-headed: the romantic atmosphere is known to inspire marriage proposals. Naturally, such a significant announcement is celebrated with a toast. The scenery, the wine and *tiempo Mendocino*, Mendoza time, the leisurely pace of those who live in this appealing region, is what visitors fondly recall; and those who stay here will smile too when they remember their days of *tiempo Cavas*.

Wine barrels at Bodega Catena Zapata

View from the lodge

Cavas Wine Lodge
Mendoza
Argentina
Tel: (54 261) 410 6927
E-mail: cecilia@cavaswinelodge.com
Internet: www.cavaswinelodge.com

Experience Management

Argentina is a word that rolls off the tongue, a name with a satisfying rhythm to it; a "four-beat bar" that echoes the staccato tempo of perhaps its most famous export – the tango.

First introduced here by immigrants in the early 1800s, the popular theory is that visiting French sailors took back the exotic dance they learned from performers in the brothels, teaching it to men and women in Europe and other parts of the world.

Whatever its origins, it has become a universally known and loved dance, with fiercely devoted fans. Amateurs, professionals and the mere admirers of the spectacle make (or want to make) a visit, almost like a pilgrimage to Buenos Aires, considered the birthplace of the tango.

Tango – the dance and the music – is pervasive here, a major part of the visitor experience. It acts as a magnet for many who want to learn the dance or work on their technique. Most of the hotels have tango teachers in-house; one free lesson is often included with your stay. The annual Tango Festival is in March: the biggest *milonga* – tango dance party – of all.

Described as a synthesis of "machismo and sexual desire, with a blend of sensitivity and aggression," the tango was historically associated with thugs, gangsters and the underclass. Now it has become gentrified, moving beyond the shady to *Dancing with the Stars* respectability.

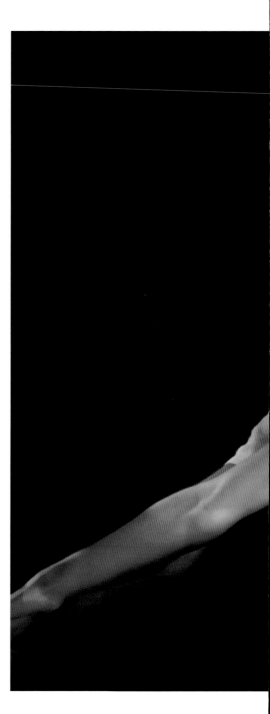

Entrance to Faena Hotel + Universe

The austere exterior belies the **opulence** within.

Just as Argentine tango is about improvisation, modifying learned steps and sequences, so too perhaps is the country. A country recovering, as it has before, from difficult times: the last in 2002, being the near collapse of its economy. Now it is rebuilding both figuratively and literally, especially in the port area Puerto Madero, alongside the Rio de la Plata – River Plate. New restaurants, cafes and apartments are coming out from the shells of rehabilitated warehouses and new constructions. This spruced-up docklands is where "starchitects" like Santiago Calatrava and Norman Foster are adding their master touches, designing bridges and buildings to provide architectural eye candy.

It is in this neighborhood that Faena Hotel + Universe has recently landed, part of an urban renewal project spearheaded by its owner, Alan Faena, first a fashion designer, now a hotel – and personal universe – developer. The hotel will be at the hub of the El Porteño Art District, a cultural quarter with art galleries and workshops, design outlets and apartments. The Faena universe is also an expanding one.

The Grand Entrance

Faena Hotel + Universe has breathed new life into what was once an old grain warehouse. There is a definite sense of arrival and anticipation as you walk along a red-carpeted runway to the stunning entrance doors. It is a good theatrical effect, one that has a showman's touch. This is the very recent stamping ground of the ubiquitous Philippe Starck, über-designer with an extensive list of hotels to his name. The Faena is one of his more playful and most comfortable styling projects. The austere exterior belies the opulence within. More is better here, with lavish touches that look back fondly to the French baroque and rococo eras. Gold swan chairs, white unicorn trophies, swags of ruby-red velvet curtains and a sequence of crystal chandeliers ornament and add flourish to what is an intriguing interior.

The Dining Room

The River Suite

The Unicorn Bistro

Young and attractive "greeters" politely direct those who walk through the Faena doors. The Grand Entrance – La Catedral in Faena-speak – looks not unlike a cathedral's nave, and as though it should always be a clear space for better effect, but in fact it is constantly busy, much like a boulevard, with people crisscrossing it to go to the restaurants, the bars, the pool or the elevators. The air is perfumed in the hall, a woody and appealing aroma lingering lightly as though some elegantly perfumed creature has just passed through. This is the Faena fragrance; the hotel has its own room scent, so that the physical atmosphere of its world is controlled and agreeable.

Faena has its own Tango Cabaret, of course; a stylish and an intimate setting for a three-course gourmet dinner and a spectacular show. While tango is more often a street experience – open-air dancing at markets or in and out of cafés especially in city quarters Recoleta and La Boca, where the dance, often described as constantly evolving, may have begun – the show tango of theaters, cabarets and clubs is more dramatically costumed and choreographed. The Faena's Tango Director, Tony Ruiz, with his musicians and team of dancers has concocted a head-spinning experience.

Bridge of the Woman, by Santiago Calatreva

You have no need to wonder what to do, or where to do it when staying here, because this is a universe with Experience Managers. Each guest is assigned an Experience Manager of their own, who may well contact you before you arrive to introduce him or herself, and ask what experiences they might help arrange for you once you are in their orbit.

Across the hall is the library bar, more like a meeting room, a private large salon, with an almost random layout that means you can sit in any one of several places. A drink at the bar, or at a small table with a light dinner, or relax down on a deep sofa ... Here you are an actor and also part of the audience, a player in the show looking on from both sides of the stage. You can be wearing a tie or a t-shirt, be young, old or in between; despite the lush surroundings there is a relaxed atmosphere. An eclectic mix of people seems to be at ease rubbing shoulders here. Diners in the very white Unicorn Bistro are likely to be more special-occasion dressers.

On this boulevard is the Faena boutique, an attraction in itself. It is one of the most interesting hotel shops there is, with an eclectic and whimsical mix of covetable objects, from miniature replicas of the room furniture to take home to your own doll's-house universe, beautiful red maté glasses and silver spoons, to great clothes that are all or mostly white, as preferred by the fashion designer — Mr. Faena himself.

A short stroll from the Faena, and fittingly near a major road, is a life-size bronze homage to an Argentine hero, Juan Manuel Fangio, the greatest Formula One driver of all time until Michael Schumacher. Gas-head historians in the known universe rate Fangio as an almost supernatural driver, "an artist in the cockpit." Clever product placement can be seen in the background: a company that was one of his original sponsors.

Most guests will venture forth from the Faena's fabulously rarified environment to experience the city and its environs; such as the shopping – there are still some bargain prices for quality goods to be had here, when compared to many other currencies – trying out the myriad of great restaurants and visiting the numerous sights, museums and galleries. Few seem to know that Buenos Aires is home to Tierra Santa, a theme park of biblical proportions. This is the Holy Land, the local one that is, near the airport. It is very like a 1950s movie set, where actors costumed as Delilah, Salome, Moses or St. Peter can be seen. Scenes from the New Testament are staged; replicas of marketplaces, streets, palaces and Golgotha complete with townspeople, slaves and Roman soldiers form the backdrop. Theme restaurants cater for the hungry, with Arabian and Armenian food. Free car parking is a blessing.

In a parallel and ideal universe, there would be Experience Managers for each of us. In the meanwhile, it is exclusive to fortunate Faena guests.

Fangio in bronze

Faena Hotel + Universe
Buenos Aires
Argentina
Tel: (54 11) 4010 9000
Fax: (54 11) 4010 9007
E-mail: info@faenaexperience.com
Internet: www.faenahotelanduniverse.com

In a Grain of Sand

Bab al Shams Desert Resort & Spa Dubai, United Arab Emirates

Deserts are perhaps the toughest of all the natural environments on earth. Harsh and barren, generally inhospitable to humans, they give sustenance to little but the most basic plant and animal life. However, they do provide some of the most spectacular scenery on our planet. In the Arabian Gulf, vision, wealth and technology are being harnessed together to construct an astonishing New World on the shifting desert sands.

One of the first of many billboards we saw lining the roads on the drive out of Dubai was for a construction company, promoting that they are "building the nation." It soon seems that should be more plural than singular. In the desert camped at the gates of the glittering city, herds of trucks are circling and tracking around massive construction projects, night and day, like animals in a game park. Giant façades show artist concepts for fantasylands – "sunny pleasure domes with caves of ice" – that are being created; a "Dubailand" that it is decreed will be the most ambitious leisure and entertainment destination ever made to measure over thousands of acres. The Seven Wonders of the World will be duplicated and handily clustered together here with shopping and indoor skiing as extra features, along with parking for thousands of cars.

Ata Allah—"God's gift"— is the Bedouin name for *Camelus dromedarius*, the Arabian camel. Perfectly adapted to desert life, camels are valued now more as thoroughbred racing animals and sentimental images of the past than as the mainstay of transportation. The limousines of Europe, Asia and America have long since taken over that role in this oil-rich federation.

A reflective pool

A desert experience with the **comfort and luxury** that such a harsh and **unforgiving landscape** rarely delivers.

High temperatures, lack of water and shortage of food are the main obstacles to survival in the desert. All of these are expertly dealt with at Jumeirah Bab al Shams Desert Resort & Spa. Its name translates to the "gateway to the sun"; this low-rise retreat basks in a desert landscape. For now it is far from the city, although like sand dunes, that too is moving, expanding as Dubai builds bigger and biggest, both up and out.

Fringed with palm trees, generously water-featured, Bab al Shams is where you will have a desert experience with the comfort and luxury that such a harsh and unforgiving landscape rarely delivers. Its architecture is derived from the traditional Arabic, an ancient walled fortress village newly interpreted. Optical illusions are a specialty of Dubai. The pools are not a mirage, though they stretch into infinity by design; neither are the lush gardens. Stone courtyards and staircases connect and lead to suites, restaurants and rooftop bars. You can lie on cushioned terraces, watch the sunset and puff on apple *shisha* under the stars. It is rustic in look but not in fact; the rooms are simply luxurious, the bathroom worthy of a movie set.

The resort is on several "hot lists": for its design and location, not for the summer temperatures, when it can reach well over 100°F (38°C). In midsummer, when we were briefly outside in sweltering dry 104°F (40°C) heat, it felt as though a huge fan heater had been left on by mistake. Inside is a welcome chill-out zone, as is the Satori Spa.

Arabian hospitality extends to a generous breakfast that includes regional specialities, and a choice of restaurants offering diverse cuisines.

One comfort likely to be difficult to find for an inexperienced passenger is riding on the back of a camel, but there are alternatives: horseback or four-wheel drives into the desert. On the sand dunes in the early evening, much-prized falcons show off their hunting skills in a display of avian acrobatics. Watching the magnificent bird, its cruel, beautiful head hooded when on its handler's arm but uncovered to soar high above the desert and dive low after its prey is better than watching an air show. Although the traditional sport of hunting with falcons is banned in most of the UAE, the bird is a pervasive emblem. Its image is printed on the federation's money, and is deemed so valuable that each registered falcon has to have its own identification. In an effort to stop illegal trading, none can be taken out of the country unless their owners can show the Falcon Passport.

Entrance hall

Arriving at Bab al Shams

Arabian lights

The rooftop bar   View of a suite

On a cool night you can walk out across the dunes, or be whisked on a buggy to Al Hadheerah, the resort's signature open-air restaurant. Inside its rock walls is lively Arabic music and entertainment – bands and belly dancers – and tastebud tempting ethnic cuisines from the diverse Arab world, cooked to order on wood-fired stone ovens and spit roasts. Lounging on cushions on the *majlis*, sunken seating, looking up at the sudden sight of a gleaming white Arabian horse poised and spot lit high on a dune above, you may have your own prince or princess of the desert *caravanserai* fantasy.

If you feel like a change from desert sand, there is a shuttle service from Bab al Shams to the beach, only 35 minutes away at the resort's sister properties; Burj al Arab, the Jumeirah Beach hotel and Madinat Jumeriah. Watersports, snow-skiing, shopping malls and *souks*; all are in reach of a short drive.

Bab al Shams is close to the Dubai International Endurance City, the headquarters for a grueling annual event where horses and riders take on a six-stage, 100 mile (160 km) race across the UAE's punishing desert terrain. At the resort, you are secluded from such or any really demanding effort. There is little endurance required to stay here; the peace and quiet of this lush desert "island" will soon restore your stamina levels.

Precious water feature

The infinity pool

A peregrine falcon and its handler

Bab al Shams Desert Resort & Spa
Dubai
United Arab Emirates

Tel: (971 4) 832 6699
Fax: (971 4) 832 6698
E-mail: JBASfeedback@jumeirah.com
Internet: www.jumeirahbabalshams.com

Supernova

Burj al Arab / Dubai, United Arab Emirates

At night, the multitude of buildings under construction in Dubai are just silhouettes in the darkness. Lit up, though, are the congregations of cranes. They look like weird skeletal Meccano birds, feeding on the frames they perch on top of. It is said that one-fifth of the world's largest cranes are in Dubai, hoisting floors higher and higher as the city literally reaches for most elevated status. Structural expressionism is definitely the ascendant architectural style here.

Worldwide, its most famous example is Burj al Arab, in English and in truth an Arabian Tower, standing many heads and shoulders above its neighbors. When architect Tom Wills-Wright was asked to submit designs for what was to be a landmark building on the Dubai skyline, he and the creative team reviewed other iconic buildings – the Sydney Opera House, the Eiffel Tower, the Pyramids – around the world. All have an unusual shape, so it was clear that for this new one to really catch the eye and imagination, it must have a remarkable form. Burj al Arab launched in 1999, and people have been looking up to it ever since.

The high-impact, high-altitude atrium is central to the prestigious hotel s unique design. It takes up a third of the interior space; with a height of 597 feet (182 m) it could shelter the Statue of Liberty. Its architect cites this as one of his favorite places; he likes to see people standing and staring up, or looking down to the lobby far below, amazed.

Burj al Arab viewed from the Jumeirah Madinat hotel

Far-sighted as falcons,
they looked down another future.
W.H. Auden

Naturally, interior designer Ms. Kuan Chew wanted to continue the "wow effect" of the building inside, and deliver the timeless and unusual concept requested. The interior was viewed as radical when the hotel opened, its dazzling decoration making it an exuberant partner to the attention-attracting façade.

Then, in that era of minimalism, eschewing decorativeness, it would have been a surprise, a shock even, to see the great soundshell-like curves framing the reception desks, and the gold columns, curling gold garlands and silver-mirrored rails that frame the first five floors of the atrium.

Entrance to Al Mahara Seafood Restaurant

Glamour in the atrium

Colors of carpets and furnishings are vibrant and rich, not muted and pale. Pattern is conspicuous. The fact that thousands of square feet of 22-karat gold leaf have been used in the interior was met with astonishment.

To this recent viewer, the overall effect is stunning; a glamorous, even futuristic interior that appeals for its lively opulence and brave use of color within such an ethereal yet masterfully engineered white spire.

Water is a central feature; dancing arcs of it weave together in a graceful display, a jet of water shoots skyward, 138 feet (42 m) high. A waterfall cascades between the escalators to the atrium lounge in an artfully computer-choreographed sequence of mesmerizing movements. Even more captivating is the underwater-themed restaurant. Access is via a three-minute virtual submarine voyage. Once you disembark, you will dine on award-winning fare, seated beside the diverse sealife of the Arabian Gulf: leopard and reef sharks, manta rays, moray eels, butterfly, unicorn and parrot fish swimming in a massive floor-to-ceiling aquarium that wraps around the hotel's signature restaurant.

Detail of a deluxe suite

Looking up into the atrium

The billowing sail of a traditional Arabian dhow was chosen as the essence of the design, transforming five years later into a spectacular hotel. Currently the world's tallest hotel, it soars 1,053 feet (321 m) into the air. A helipad cantilevered out from its top floor has also served as a grass tennis court for Andre Agassi and Roger Federer, and a green for Tiger Woods. The sail's translucent white fabric is actually Teflon-coated fiberglass, stretched across the steel structural frame. By day the glow of the white wall lights up the atrium; at night, the facade becomes a beacon, with a kinetic display of light in changing colors. Fire and water shows make an even greater spectacle.

Not long after Burj al Arab opened, an understandably enthusiastic journalist reported that her stay here was a "seven-star" experience. Although in fact the hotel is rated the highest of the star system at five-plus, it is indeed in a different galaxy in terms of its innovative design, its luxury suites, butler service and spa, and its ability to impress even the most jaded. It has become the pin-up poster of destination architecture.

View from Al Muntaha Sky View Restaurant 650 feet (200 m) metres above the Arabian Gulf

Souk Madinat Jumeirah shopping center

A new Colossus of Dubai is taking shape. Currently under construction, Burj Dubai is a 2,650 foot (808 m) – and could be even higher – skyscraper designed by architects Skidmore, Owings and Merrill. When completed, it will be the tallest humanmade structure of any kind in history. Standing apart on its own island, curving white against the sky, Burj al Arab will keep its title as the instantly recognizable and iconic building on the Dubai skyline.

Burj al Arab
Dubai
United Arab Emirates

Tel: (971 4) 301 7777
Fax: (971 4) 301 7000
E-mail: BAAinfo@jumeirah.com
Internet: www.burj-al-arab.com

Australian Gold

| The Adelphi Hotel | Melbourne, Australia |

Melbourne is the only Southern Hemisphere city on the Formula One car racing circuit. To the delight of many and annoyance of some, the track is close to the center of the city, and the noise of the FI cars roars across town for three days. The Grand Prix, opening the motor-racing season's international calendar, is followed by the much quieter Wine and Food Festival.

The Melbourne city skyline
from across the Yarra River

The Adelphi Hotel

Later in the year, more horsepower of a different kind fires up the city. The Melbourne Cup is Australia's take on England's Ascot Week, attracting racing enthusiasts and partygoers to see thoroughbreds gallop their stuff.

These two major events add a sporty flavor to a city that has claimed to be the Australian capital of arts and culture. Nicknamed the "Milan of the South Pacific," Melbourne is an urbane city once considered conservative, now called cosmopolitan.

Going off the deep end is not behavior to be recommended at the Adelphi. This hotel, designed and owned by cutting-edge Australian architects Denton Corker Marshall, was their response to a self-set brief: to create a

A deluxe room

Minimalist en-suite

place that they themselves would want to stay in. For years the result, set in a refurbished 1930s building, was the only good hotel in an alternative contemporary style. Deliberately stark, in the heart of the central city, it is more like a club than a hotel.

One of its most remarked-on features is the literally over-the-top swimming pool. This is a glass-bottomed lap pool with a difference, for it juts several feet beyond the edge of the hotel roof, giving swimmers a surreal view of the street below. Kick too vigorously and you can send water spilling over onto the heads of unsuspecting passersby, who are puzzled by a seemingly localized rain shower. There is a weird sense of suspension for the swimmer doing the Australian crawl out across the cantilevered edge.

The hotel's rooftop bar overlooks the pool, the twin-spired Cathedral, and across to the Edwardian dome of the Flinders Street Railway Station.

The Adelphi's furnishings are under the influence of the Memphis school of design to some degree. The bold clean design with bright colors and sharp edges has the architects' trademark oblique angles. Some of the sharp edges of tables have had shin protectors, affectionately called Avant Guards, fitted after a few guests claimed the furniture walked into them.

Rooftop exterior

The minimalist bathrooms of granite and white translucent glass seem larger than they are due to maximum mirror use.

All the furniture and rugs were designed by the architect-owners. They also designed the modernist entranceway to the city. Affectionately known to locals as the "Big Zipper," this red and yellow sculpture protrudes over the motorway. Their predilection for cantileverage is evident on DCM's Melbourne Exhibition Centre as well, a distinctive building on the skyline.

The Adelphi is right in the heart of Melbourne, a short walk to theaters, cinemas, restaurants, bars and shopping. Hairy Canary and the Gin Palace, bar-restaurants, are neighbors in the same street. Langton's Restaurant and Wine Bar is in the next lane, a fortunate location.

Close by is the Southbank area, an elegant promenade alongside the Yarra River, complete with mega-casino, great cafés, bars and name fashion labels.

Melbourne is one of the few places left where trams are still a major mode of transport, and its City Circle tram circumnavigates the center for effortless sightseeing.

The influence of the many immigrants who have settled in Melbourne is most obvious in the cosmopolitan cuisine available – from Italian to Vietnamese – and the world-class wines.

Melbourne is also a city with a sense of humor. Its Comedy Festival is one of the annual highlights in an action-packed calendar of events that lure more and more visitors there each year.

The pool jutting a few feet over the edge

The Adelphi Hotel

Melbourne
Australia

Tel: (61 3) 9650 7555
Fax: (61 3) 9650 2710
E-mail: info@adelphi.com.au
Internet: www.adelphi.com.au

No Worries

Daintree Eco Lodge & Spa | Daintree, Australia

There are only two types of weather here: perfect and beautiful. That's the catchphrase of North Queensland, and is the response you will often get when you ask a local what the weather forecast is for the next day.

This is the wet tropics, with rainforest that is older than the Amazon rainforest by around 40 million years. It is fiercely green wherever you look, thick, interlaced and luxuriant, highlighted with a splash of red or yellow, white or blue – flowers, fruits, birds: perhaps an azure kingfisher, a yellow-breasted figbird or a rainbow bee-eater perched in the dark, shady canopy. It is perfumed with whatever is in flower; ylang-ylang, native jasmine, wattle – sometimes with an undernote of rich decay, not surprising when you consider that this is primeval forest. One of the most naturally diverse places on our planet, this World Heritage area is home to one-third of Australia's marsupials, including a very odd variety of kangaroo. The rare Lumholtz's tree kangaroo can not only climb trees but also travel backward. They are not often or easily seen in their natural habitat.

Bats, frogs, crocodiles, butterflies and the world's largest moth – Hercules – call this home. Over half the bird population of Australia is here. One is the wompoo fruit dove, a large, beautiful green bird, and the emblem of the Daintree Eco Lodge & Spa, often heard but not seen camouflaged in the deep forest setting.

Julaymba Restaurant and Art Gallery

A koala bear

You can become a tree person for a few nights, high up in a comfortable treehouse of your own set in the canopy of this rainforest retreat, "at one with nature," yet with all the creature comforts that we humans like. Several of the long-legged villas have a Jacuzzi on the balcony, private although some bird and animal eyes will doubtless spot you. This is a birdwatcher's heaven. You look out to soft filtered daylight and listen to a symphonic chorus of frogs, birds and insects.

Interior of Villa 11, *Karrkul* – a green "adorable" frog.

On your arrival at the Daintree Eco Lodge, nestled in 30 acres of its own lush rainforest valley, you will be given a piece of jewelry and encouraged to wear it while you are here. Attached to a leather cord is a "burnie" bead, a seed painted in the distinctive and decorative dotwork style that is key to Aboriginal art. It is yours to keep, as a memento of your stay, and a sign of a most important tenet here. Aboriginal culture is a major part of the Daintree Eco Lodge experience. Elders of the local Kuku Yalanji Aboriginal community named each villa after a creature in the forest. The Aboriginal guides offer guests the chance to understand their ancient and complex culture, founded on harmony between people and the land, with guided rainforest walks through giant ferns and bushtucker hunts – looking for indigenous food and medicine sources – as well as Aboriginal arts and craft classes. Part of the indoor dining room is a gallery of Aboriginal art.

Villas in the rainforest

Aboriginal culture is a major part of the Daintree Eco Lodge experience.

This is a place of tranquillity and reflection, and at its heart is the spa, now practically a given wherever you stay. But this one has a real point of difference in that it is very much linked to the place it is in. The rainforest Aboriginal people gave this spot the name *Wawu-karrba* – meaning a place of healing of the spirit. Traditions from their spiritual and material world are carefully blended with orthodox spa treatments resulting in an unusual and unique therapy menu, rightfully award-winning. Much dreamtime can be spent here in blissful hours that refresh mind and body. At the head of the cool, green valley there is a waterfall: the source of all the pristine spring water needed for the property, another site-specific advantage in this drought-prone country. Aboriginals respect waterfalls as women's places, and so it has become an extension of the spa, a secluded place for outdoor bathing treatments that are truly natural, and at other times a place to walk to and rest. The environment is restorative, and the Julaymba restaurant is part of the potent mix. Overlooking a freshwater lagoon, it is reached by boardwalks threaded through the rainforest and serves contemporary Australian food with inventive twists, featuring native fruits and berries.

Barretts Creek

The southern cassowary bird

Water is an integral theme at the lodge, from the spa's rain shower to the soothing constant sound of the stream in the valley. In keeping with that, it is just a short walk across to the Daintree River, where you can join author Dan Irby on his mangrove adventure tour. A boat trip with Dan in the early morning, during the day or at sunset will take you and a few others up Barretts Creek into the mangrove delta to see the rich plant, animal and bird life along the isolated waterways. The rainforest is lush here. Great Tarzan-like vines loop across the river like bridges. Sunlight falls down like streaks of white paint onto the green below. Massive mangrove roots hidden in the shadows of the bank are suddenly lit up by a sunray; a graceful white egret takes flight or a brahminy kite soars overhead.

Slow down signs

Estaurine crocodiles lie craftily obscured on riverbanks. Roadside signs everywhere near water warn this is a crocodile area and dangerous; from December to March they are nesting and very aggressive. Rare plants that can only survive in highly oxyengated environments flourish here, and strange birds, like the southern cassowary, a huge bizarre and severe looking creature that appears to be wearing a curious helmet, almost ecclesiastic in its design. Solitary, flightless and often run over by speeding drivers, it is an endangered species. Its uncertain future is of special concern given its importance to rainforest diversity. Cassowaries are the only animals capable of distributing the seeds of more than 70 species of trees whose fruit is too large for any other forest dwelling animal to eat and move.

Coral sand beaches or the Great Barrier Reef beckon for day trips. Or you can go across the river on the cable ferry and drive up the rugged coast further north to Cape Tribulation, another of the cheerful names bestowed by Captain Cook marking his experiences in the Pacific. In 1770 his ship ran hard upon a coral reef off the coast, earning the cape its English name. Here beaches and rainforest meet in a beautiful, lonely landscape with few people. The Daintree Ice-cream Company is along this road, making gourmet tastes from native seeds and fruits. It was a doubly worthwhile stop as this was where we saw our first cassowary bird, high-stepping quickly across the grass through the trees away from its surprised but spellbound public.

One of the most prevalent Australian phrases neatly describes the laid-back atmosphere up in the Daintree. "No worries" is what you will have here, and what concerns you have brought with you can be soothed away at least for a time at the lodge and in the spa.

A mangrove lake

Daintree Eco Lodge & Spa
Daintree
Australia

Tel: (61 7) 4098 6100
Fax: (61 7) 4098 6200
E-mail: info@daintree-ecolodge.com.au
Internet: www.daintree-ecolodge.com.au

Rock Star

Voyages Longitude 131° / Ayers Rock, Australia

Unquestionably this is the main attraction, the headline act at any given time in Central Australia; Uluṟu, a giant rockberg. Far more is hidden under the ground than the great sandstone solidity that rises out of the surrounding red desert.

Rock-watching over a day rewards the viewer with changing colors and patterns in what could almost be a carefully choreographed light show, until after sunset, when the night completely cloaks the giant rock and it at last has privacy from the fans – until sunrise, when the next performance begins. Just before dawn, hundreds of car headlights thread through the darkness like flashlights, on their way to the show venue. The spectators gather, quiet and expectant in the early morning shadows, waiting for the curtain to go up on the day.

Geology is the scientific explanation for its existence, but its presence is such that you might imagine that Uluṟu has a purpose; a mysterious motive for being here. Photographs record its chameleon colors, give an impression of its size, but cannot transmit the atmosphere of actually being here. It has an air of majesty, and in some light and shadow effects, the folds and markings on its great sides resemble the skin of that goliath of the animal world, the elephant. From a distance, it looks as if it could be draped in cloth – you could even think it is covered in suede, perhaps another of the massive projects mounted by wrap artist Christo.

At night, with rocks hidden
and few lights to be seen,
the stars glittering
overhead are the feature.

It seems appropriate that such a wonder of natural solidity is balanced by what might appear humanmade fragility; small white tents placed at a respectful distance, like a base camp for rock fans. Set on a secluded sand dune on the edge of the Uluru-Kata Tjuta National Park, Longitude 131° is a camp, but of the luxury kind. Its setting is in a harsh environment, the Red Centre of Australia, where once only aboriginal people lived, until European explorers, emissaries, entrepreneurs and exploiters of one kind or another arrived. They too pitched tents as their Outback accommodation, but theirs were spartan shelters, certainly nothing like these ones.

The view is as spectacular now as it was then. On a straight line behind Uluru, some 20 miles (32 km) away, are the massive domes of Kata Tjuta – the Olgas – a curious conglomerate formation acting as backup singers or the band for the rock star Uluru. This is a World Heritage area, listed for its obvious natural values and its cultural meaning; the associations between the landscape and the Anangu, the traditional Aboriginal owners of the land. Their heritage is upheld through their stories and laws, their

Voyages Longitude 131° with Kata Tjuṯa in background

Tjukurpa, woven through the narratives of the tour guides. Longitude 131° has tours exclusive to its guests; walks around and through the great rocks at sunrise, sunset and during the day bring you up close to both these amazing features and the surrounding terrain.

Visually, this is quite a designer desert; it looks as though a color consultant has advised that all plain brown dirt be replaced with red earth, and then dotted with green and white flora highlights and, as a final touch, suggested may as well do the rocks red too. In fact this is not a desert; technically it is a semi-arid landscape, and surprisingly green. Juvenile forms of desert oaks sprout like bottlebrushes, fluffy standard-bearers that line the drive in to the resort and gather around it. Spinifex bushes and mulga trees, native to Australia, grow here, and sometimes wildflowers.

At night, with rocks hidden and few lights to be seen, the stars glittering overhead are the feature. Guests are treated to a candlelit dinner under their natural canopy. The Milky Way is more thickly studded and shining brighter than most of us will have seen before. As the audience gazes upward, the after-dinner speaker gives a star-talk, pointing out constellations with the aid of a startlingly powerful flashlight – its beam will surprise any residents on Alpha Centauri when it reaches it in four or so years' time. The Aboriginal people have another way of looking at the southern night sky; they focus on the spaces between the stars, naming and navigating by those. Just to have the time to stand and stare at the night sky is another of the luxuries available here.

The Dune House

A white dome roof and flowing fabric draped from the center give the illusion of camping. But unlike the early pioneers and explorers, guests under these canopies have all the creature comforts, including air conditioning for heat and cold. In the summer months, daytime temperatures outside can reach 118°F (48°C); in winter as low as 32°F (0°C).

Each of the 15 tents is named after key figures in the recent European history of Australia; from controversial explorers Burke and Wills to E.J. Conellan, the builder of Connair, Central Australia's first airline and pioneer in opening up the Red Centre to tourism, and Olive Pink, described as "the fiercest white woman in captivity," who was an artist, anthropologist, gardener and a trailblazing Aboriginal land-rights activist. Their potted biographies make interesting reading and give a more personal insight to the area. The tent walls are decorated with visual reference to their namesakes too.

Private and peaceful, these tents are ones you would like to pack up and steal away with; complete with viewing deck and furnishings – a mix of colonial and contemporary pieces, a color scheme in earthy and natural tones, and a bathroom no camp tent ever had.

There is no cooking over a campfire here; gourmet meals are served in the Dune House, the massive tented central meeting place, with a dining room, lounge and library. A swimming pool is at its base – literally between a rock and a hard place.

The tent interior

View outside the tent

Inside the Dune House

The view from each tent

The view from every tent is dominated by this amazing monolith, moored on the horizon like a giant ship. Uluru is 1,142 feet (348 m) high at its tallest point, higher than Sydney's Centrepoint Tower, New York's Chrysler Building or Burj al Arab Hotel in Dubai.

The local Anangu people do not want visitors to climb Uluru, but stop short of forbidding it. Their reasons are explained, the request is clearly made, but the final decision is left to the individual. To climb the world's largest rock is against the wishes of its traditional owners because the path you would follow is the route taken by their ancestral Mala (rufous hare-wallaby men) on their arrival at this sacred place. Just walking around the base, and seeing some of the spiritual sites is an unforgettable experience; having to see the view from the top seems somewhat unnecessary.

Longitude 131° has put a careful imprint on this landscape, ecologically aware and mindful of the spectacular wilderness setting it is fortunate to be in. Staying here is a luxury experience, in terms of the accommodation, and in what you can see. This part of Australia has been called the Never-Never; rumor has it because "they who have lived in it and loved it 'Never-Never' voluntarily leave it." Put it on your list of places to see and stay before you leave this world; of all the rock stars here on earth, this is the greatest.

The Muṯiṯjulu waterhole at Uluṟu

Voyages Longitude 131°

Ayers Rock
Australia

Tel: (61 2) 8296 8000
Fax: (61 2) 8296 8052
E-mail: travel@voyages.com.au
Internet: www.longitude131.com.au

Bliss at Blumau

The Rogner-Bad Blumau Hotel Blumau, Austria

We appear to be lost. Our taxi driver has slowed and is anxiously leaning forward to scan passing road signs. We can see his worried face reflected in the rearview mirror. Our destination is the Rogner-Bad Blumau, a spa hotel located one hour's drive south of Vienna. It is nearly dusk, and our one-hour journey is in danger of taking two as we drive through yet another picturesque village – or maybe it's the same one – in the lush green Austrian countryside.

Suddenly a sign looms – Rogner-Bad Blumau – and our relieved driver swings his carload of stressed passengers up a long winding drive toward the hotel. But we forget our irritation when we catch sight of the hotel. Located on the hillside is a surreal collection of buildings that would make even Dr. Seuss look twice. Pink castles with golden onion-domed towers, oval eye-shaped structures with grass-covered roofs, multicolored textured walls and, in the center, a steaming thermal mineral water lake.

Colorful and decorative, this hotel façade strikes a chord that wouldn't pass for architectural critique, but we are immediately amused and pleased by the contrast between this perky, exuberant building and its neatly manicured and ordered rural setting. It's visual fun. And as we were to find out, the hotel is also a place for serious relaxation and stress escape.

The House of Art, House of Bricks and the main building

Designed by Friedensreich Hundertwasser, the famous Austrian artist and architect, the Rogner-Bad Blumau Spa Hotel is an unparalleled visual experience and draw for Austria's spa district of Styria. The grassed roofs and the total absence of any straight lines give the impression that many of the buildings are growing out of the ground. Hundertwasser believes that "the straight line creates speed; speed creates stress." Perhaps this philosophy inspired our taxi driver's roundabout route.

There has been plenty of architectural criticism of both Hundertwasser and his buildings. The hotel has been aptly described as a gingerbread fantasia, and it is certainly a modern take on the baroque castle. However, as a friend once said, aren't we lucky it's there so we can criticize it. Since the Rogner-Bad Blumau opened in 1998 it has enjoyed high levels of occupancy, and is popular for weekend breaks, so it demonstrably works as a hotel. Form hasn't triumphed over function here.

The more different
things there are,
the richer the world ...

Once inside, relieved to have finally arrived, we are welcomed by smiling, sympathetic staff. Our room key is a bright blue wristwatch, a "key-bracelet," with the inscription "a life in harmony with nature." Wear this and a wave of the wrist gains entry to all the guest facilities. Much more harmonious and easier to find than a plastic key card.

Our room, high in the pink onion-topped tower, is spacious and quite plain. Its unvarnished wood and natural fabrics are certainly more sober than might be expected after the somewhat tipsy exterior. However, the sobriety is abandoned in the tiled mosaic patchwork of the bathroom. While it has the requisite fixtures and an efficient shower, its cheerful, slightly crazy atmosphere is rarely found in bathroom design.

From our windows we can see the large outdoor thermal spa pool with its silver-spout water jets. And we imagine we can hear the sea, which is puzzling since we are in landlocked Austria. An inspection reveals a second, smaller pool adjacent to the main pool. Its wave-making machine is in full swing, sending crashing waves from one end of the pool to the other, to the delight of bathers enjoying the instant surf. We rise at daybreak to photograph the sunrise. Golden early morning sunlight filters through the low mist hanging over the hotel, and at the main entrance, a group of people is busy unloading a hot air balloon. In the distance, partly hidden by mist and trees, the gothic steeple of a nearby village church glints with the rising sun.

After choosing a healthy and hearty breakfast from the enormous variety offered, we wander the tiled hallways connecting the therapy treatment rooms of the Holistic Health Institute. Guests traverse these hallways on their way to and from the various treatments, usually dressed in robes and slippers supplied by the hotel. This is a state-of-the-art health spa as well as an architectural whimsy on a grand scale; delighting the eye and senses as it restores the spirit.

The outdoor pool

Eco-friendly bedroom 1502

The mosaic tiled bathroom

Many different stress-relieving treatments are available, from computer-controlled water-massage baths to advanced dietary treatments, but it was the music and sound therapy that intrigued us. Initially doubtful of its worth, we listened to the description of this therapy with raised eyebrows. The experience proved the better test. The therapy was developed by Wolfgang Koelbl, a holistic doctor, and it is unique to the Rogner-Bad Blumau. The recipient lies on a couch, which has an instrument like a xylophone underneath it. This is strummed, allowing both sound and vibration to soothe the mind. Added to this are several layers of additional sounds, using instruments such as the monochord, Tibetan singing bowls, and brass gongs and a sound pyramid. Sound therapy was used in traditional Tibetan healing and by the Incas, and Dr. Koelbl believes music is the path to the inner self. Cynical at first, we both rose from the couch feeling uplifted and relaxed, our heads ringing with the beautiful and unusual sounds.

The centerpiece of Rogner-Bad Blumau is the thermal pool with its restorative healing properties. Massaging water jets are strategically placed around the edges and at the center of the pool, bliss for a travel-weary body.

It is best to visit the pool at twilight, lying in the warm spa water and watching the sun go down before swimming through a short tunnel into the indoor pool. You can relax even further stretched out on a chaise then eat poolside or amble on to a leisurely dinner.

The two restaurants serve great food and wine, which say more about good living than the spa environment – and there are no watchful calorie-counting attendants disguised as waiters to catch you unawares.

Sound and music therapy

Hot-air balloon with eye-shaped house and main building in background

I think the onion shape
means richness and happiness;
wealth, opulence and fertility.

Go to this "oasis of wellness" to relax, recuperate and be amused by the witty environment. During our stay, we didn't leave the hotel and its immediate surroundings, but there is much to do besides just "spa-ing out." Activities include golf, ballooning and horseback riding.

Restored and inspired, we boarded a hotel shuttle van headed for Vienna airport. Driving off, my last glance of the hotel through the rear window was to reassure myself that the three-day experience, staying in what may well be the world's first inhabitable work of art, was not just imaginary.

Wall of the House of Art

Rogner-Bad Blumau Hotel
Blumau
Austria

Tel: (43) 3383 5100-0
Fax: (43) 3383 5100-808
E-mail: resm@blum.rogner.co.at
Internet: www.rogner.com

Welcome to Africa

Sandibe Safari Lodge / Okavango Delta, Botswana

Charge of the heavy brigade

Our arrival in Africa was the cause of some considerable irritation to the largest land creature on the planet. Within 10 minutes of landing at the small dusty airstrip in Botswana's Okavango Delta and on our way to the lodge, it was made very clear by this major representative of the animal kingdom that our stay would only be tolerated on his terms.

"Leave only footprints" is the motto of CC Africa, the owners of eco-tourism Sandibe Safari Lodge, and for a few seconds we wondered whether footprints would be all that was left of us – if we were foolish enough to make a run for it, away from the charging bull elephant. Of course, as our savvy driver Sage pointed out, we could not outrun an animal that can go from 0–15 mph (0–25 km/h) in about three seconds. He reversed the Land-Cruiser as the magnificent beast began its run and we made a hasty retreat. Thank you Sage and Toyota.

Surprised by such an immediate and dramatic interaction with the animals we had come to see, I thought as I watched the temper display that it seemed too soon into this long-anticipated trip for it to end in disaster. Afterward, the photographer admitted his only real fear was that he might not get a great photo of the charge. All that's missing are the sound effects.

Of course we were in no real danger; the experienced Sandibe rangers know when it is best to retreat from any likely confrontation with wildlife. This not a zoo, there are no fences; animals roam free where they will. That roaming may be across your path. They have the right of way, not you.

Dining outdoors

Its almost silent passing is the more startling because its **sheer size** would make it seem noisier.

Our arrival and welcome at Sandibe was a relief after two days of traveling to get here. We had been feeling weary, but we were wide awake now. An encounter with an angry elephant is a sure-fire antidote to jet lag, but regrettably not available in tablet form. Lured by the legend of Africa, the great, terrible and fabulous history of the continent, and to this country partly by the evocative charming stories set in Botswana by author Alexander McCall Smith, it felt both strange and familiar to finally be here.

The camp's architecture mimics its organic forest setting, the lodge and guest cottages built in a natural clearing. Jackalberry and fig trees shade the camp from the sun, and the view is out over tall reed grasses and the Santantebi River. The thatched roof cottages are spacious, very comfortable and decorated in an attractive fusion of textiles; silk and leather, with woven mats, copper and rough-hewn wood. Each cottage has its own game-viewing deck, almost in a tree. Laundry service is of course available, but it has a different challenge here: baboons might raid the washing line. You could see your designer shirt swinging through the trees.

It was August, warm during the day but comfortably so, cool at night and early morning. As we enjoy pre-dinner drinks on the terrace, conversation is suddenly stilled as a large dark shape looms into view in the shadows just

Entrance to Sandibe

Cottage interior

beyond our raised platform. Glasses in hand, we watch, motionless, as a great elephant moves slowly past us. Its almost silent passing is the more startling because its sheer size would make it seem noisier. This elephant ignores us, intent on its relentless search for food, skirts the nearby dining table, and walks out of sight.

Dinner at Sandibe is often served outdoors, in a *boma*, a lantern-lit clearing. The food is described as pan-African cuisine, we voted it delicious, so much so I bought the book *A Kitchen Safari*, recipes seasoned with great photographs. A three-course dinner with wine is a good precursor to a deep sleep. It will be an early morning start the next day.

Just before sunrise the wakeup call is a soft beating of a drum outside your door. In less than an hour, you will be on a game drive, out of your comfortable bed and into a rough-rider vehicle that goes offroad into the bush and through the magnificent wetland wilderness of the Delta. Our ranger M.K. is the driver, and riding out on the spotter's chair is James, the tracker, both constantly scanning the landscape for signs of life. Their experienced and sharp eyes see far and first what else is on the move.

Lodge interior

The wildlife you will very likely see in this free-range animal environment are *kudu* – graceful antelopes – giraffes, lions, hippos, crocodiles and a host of birds. Elephant are plentiful; protecting them from poachers has been successful. Their increasing numbers cut a destructive swathe through the landscape as they range far and wide to feed their giant frames. As we observe close up, the bird and animal life cycle is a primal chain of what eats what and when. Feeding time is most of the time: this is really a huge restaurant, self-service only, and you too could be on the menu.

Some drives you may see few of the big animals, perhaps none – the unpredictability of it is part of being in their natural habitat. Whether you see a stealthy lioness, perhaps only feet from where you are sitting in the vehicle, or a great hippo surface in the water as you are having morning tea on the riverbank, or nothing bigger than a flashy kingfisher, only adds a fascinating edge to the experience.

Another mode of transport is a *mokoro*, a dugout canoe, in which you are poled along the waterways, gliding through water lilies and reeds, a dragonfly skimming the surface ahead, above an African fish eagle, on the horizon the sun slowly descending. In the gold light of early evening this voyage is magical, one you will remember when you are back home on a congested highway.

On our last night at the camp we were treated to a performance of singing and dancing by the entire camp team. Their harmonious voices lifted up into the night air, adding to the many surround sounds of Africa.

The exciting start to our African visit fit the cliché that "it is better to travel hopefully than to arrive." We enjoyed the arrival far more than the journey, and the ensuing experience of Sandibe. *Pula* is the Botwana word for "rain" and also "money," both valued currencies, and so it is the usual toast made there to raise your glass in celebration. *Pula* to Sandibe; with luck we will be back.

Elephant close-up

Baobab tree

Waterway travel by *mokoro*

Hippopotamus

Lioness on the hunt

Sandibe Safari Lodge

Okavango Delta
Botswana, Africa

Tel: (27 11) 809-4300
E-mail: inquiries@ccafrica.com
internet: www.sandibe.com

War and Peace

Amansara / Siem Reap, Cambodia

There is a fight to the death going on here; tree and stone locked in mortal combat. All in silence. Not even the sound of birds in this darkly lit place. Among these graphic scenes of battle, the only effect missing is the noise of the struggle. There are many places where the wood has won, bursting through the ancient temple walls and roof, then crouching over the final collapse. Tree roots flow like a mass of snakes over walls and through doorways.

There is a powerful force here, the sense of some impenetrable mystery hidden in the shadows. Eerie in early morning half-light, absolute quiet, no other living thing among the vestiges of a once magnificent monastery, we can imagine how that first French explorer was struck speechless with astonishment when he came upon the labyrinthine temples of Angkor more than a century ago. The scene is almost theatrical in its state of decay. Then, suddenly, there is movement, noise and voices. Others are here. We have been whispering with our guide, now we are back in real time.

Right: The monastery of Ta Prohm

The dining room

In Cambodia, the traditional form of greeting is the *sompeyar*, a gracious gesture of politeness and respect. Hands placed palms together and held upward, the head inclined slightly forward, often paired with a slight bow, nearly always with a gentle smile. This is our welcome to the house of Amansara, a peaceful retreat on the road to Angkor, the cultural heart of the Kingdom of Cambodia.

There is an immediate sense of place, arriving at Siem Reap. The interior of its pagoda-style airport terminal is almost elegant in its design. A large Buddha is seated on a white stone elephant, with beautiful silk lanterns overhead. We are driven to our destination in a gleaming black Mercedes saloon, vintage 60s, through the busy streets of the rapidly expanding little town. Hotels and restaurants have sprung up here as visitors arrive in increasing numbers. The recent return of comparative normality and peace after wartorn decades has put Cambodia back on the traveler's agenda. Angkor is its prime architectural and historical treasure. A monumental expression of the golden age of Khmer civilization, the ancient temples are just minutes from Amansara. Hidden behind high walls is a 60s modernist treasure, originally King Norodom Sihanouk's own villa. Dignitaries and celebrities were hosted at the royal retreat in those halcyon days. Later it became an exclusive hotel, until the dark-age advent of the Khmer Rouge in the 70s. After occupation by the military during the 1980s, it reopened in 1992.

A pool suite

Ten years later, Amanresorts bought and respectfully restored it, adding new suites and a spa. Now the former royal enclave is a patrician luxury resort, a peaceful haven that lives up to the meaning of its name. The scent of flowers hangs lightly in the tranquil air of Amansara; the courtyard gardens are full of exotic blooms; manicured lawns are richly green set against the white buildings.

Detail of pool suite interior

Bicycles at Amansara

Its lotus-bud towers
show its Indian inspiration.

The suites are a fusion of culture and comfort. Playing in the background is the Lama's Chant, hypnotic music with murmuring conversation, "Songs of Awakening" that could contribute to the trance-like state you may well enter into, cocooned in this serenely elegant environment.

The holy structure of Angkor Wat was built on the order of Cambodian king Jayavaran around the 12th century; originally in veneration to the Hindu god Vishnu, but later converted to Buddhist use. Its lotus-bud towers show its Indian inspiration. A statement of wealth and power, abandoned and then invaded over the centuries by the jungle, Angkor Wat is an enduring national symbol. Its silhouette is everywhere: on the Cambodian flag, numberplates, stamps and more. All the temples of Angkor suffered little damage during the recent civil wars.

Not so the artists of Cambodia: only 10 percent survived the murderous Pol Pot era. A renewal of Cambodian performing art is taking place. One spectacular cultural piece in the Amansara repertoire is *sbaek thom*, an ancient and rare form of shadow puppetry. The large puppets are each made from one cow skin and intricately patterned; all the players are dancers too. Beautiful against the firelight, the dramatic shadows on the screen tell of a heroic episode from the Ramayana, the arduous rescue of a kidnapped queen.

Angkor Wat

Shadow puppetry

The swimming pool

While Angkor Wat is the centerpiece of the Angkor archaeological park, there are many other remarkable temples; some 300 of the 1,000 or so in Cambodia are here in Siem Reap. As well as the ruins of the past, there is a present-day world beyond the Amansara gates. A trip to the food market, dining at authentic and eccentric restaurants, visiting the floating village and flooded forest on Tonle Sap lake are recommended on their top 10 list. Would that we had more time.

The remork fleet   Buddha at Angkor Wat

Amansara nourishes your mental and physical well-being within its walls, either in the dining room or the spa. There is a dual menu of "home" food – western style – and Khmer dishes, which you can choose between or combine; all are simply delicious. On the treatment menu in the stunningly designed spa is the foot cooler: "no doubt you thanked your guide for taking you around the temples, why not thank your feet for doing the same. We bathe them, scrub them and massage them … " After that, you can put them up in the library, where the collection of books could slow even a speed-reader for a few days. The lap pool will exercise the energetic; the languid will stay beside the curved pool or in the privacy of their room's own water features.

Amansara takes care of everything for temple visiting. Their own guides will take you on secluded paths to enter the temples at dawn, while the driver of your *remork* waits to bring you home. Our guide tells us he was the location scout for the movie *Lara Croft, Tomb Raider*; where sets were built and scenes created, what Angelina Jolie was like – very nice – and that many people come here now to make films. He also recounts, briefly and in a direct tone, his own story, forced as a young boy like many others to collaborate with the Khmer Rouge. Travel to a place like this can make clear a fact very well known to much of the world's population: life is truly a fragile thing. To be able to voyage to Amansara and see the legacy of a long-ago civilization is our great fortune; we wish Cambodia good luck and a peaceful future.

Amansara
Siem Reap
Cambodia
Tel: (855) 63 760 333
Fax: (855) 63 760 335
E-mail: amansara@amanresorts.com
Internet: www.amansara.com

Illustrious Energy

The handsome vintage 1934 Rolls-Royce Phantom II drawn up beside the hotel is kept polished and pristine. Its great age merely makes it all the more valuable. The pride of the fleet, its distinguished appearance is certain to create attention.

It earns more than admiring glances. At the 2006 Hong Kong Classic Car Show it won the "most desirable car" vote. But it is not just a showpiece; rather a working member of a regiment of younger Rolls-Royces, 14 Silver Spurs all painted in a distinctive shade known as "Peninsula green," a color unique to the Peninsula Hotel, where they are the transport of choice. Guests can settle back in their luxurious interiors and travel to or from the airport in a gracious style to which some may already be accustomed, and that others will enjoy as a special treat. Or you may prefer a more modern mode. In that case, by helicopter direct to the 28th floor can be your arrival and departure point, where you will be ushered through to the privacy and comfort of the heli-passenger-only China Clipper club.

The more usual entry point is through the front doors. Coolness and warmth mix like an ocean current, from the moment when the white-clad smiling pageboy opens the door, and you leave the sultry heat and exchange it for the regulated temperature and dignified elegance of the Peninsula lobby.

The atmosphere is not hushed but courtly, **graciously welcoming** you into its portals.

The sense of moving from a vibrant, even chaotic city outside to a calm and soothing environment is palpable. Entering the massive gilded lobby, you are greeted by the sight of a grand old hotel still in its heyday.

Classic colonial it may be, but the luxurious space of its foyer alone is impressive and its Old World decorativeness beautiful. First opened in 1928, then the first and only luxury hotel in Hong Kong, now the oldest, it is still its grandest. The atmosphere is not hushed but courtly, graciously welcoming you into its portals. Afternoon tea is served in the Lobby, an out-of-Empire custom that attracts so many people that every day a thousand scones are baked as one of the expected traditional comestibles. Sandwiches and cakes are delivered on tiered stands by quietly attentive waiters to tables set with silverware and china, a special blend from the Peninsula tea collection is poured; tea taken in a relaxed elegant atmosphere that makes it a quite special and for many a novel experience.

View across Victoria Harbour

So popular is it that orderly lineups begin to form discreetly behind the potted palms quite soon after midday. However, dignified does not mean dull; while retaining its old-style glamour, the Peninsula has kept pace with contemporary standards. From the standard but deluxe guest rooms through to the stunning suites, furnishings and fixtures should meet and likely exceed the expectations of the most discerning guests. Classy décor, state of the art technology, and often a spectacular view of one of the world's most stunning cityscapes are a heady mix. You can go higher, to the rooftop, for drinks, dinner and dancing at Felix. It is a choreographed arrival in a glamorous dark-chocolate-experience elevator; as you near the 28th floor, the elevator lights fade, making the dramatic impact greater when you enter the restaurant. Created by Philippe Starck, an often theatrical designer, it is a clever contemporary contrast to the classic lobby far below and an example of the adaptive skills of the Peninsula.

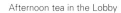

Afternoon tea in the Lobby

View of the Peninsula

The Peninsula Suite

The swimming pool

Of course, there is a state-of-the-art spa, and fitness center with a glamorous pool; both play a part of the Peninsula Wellness lifestyle program offered as an antidote to the stress and strains caused by the hectic pace of modern life. Indulgence can be all-inclusive here. There are six different restaurants in the hotel, and all-day dining in the Lobby, and you can have a culinary experience at the Peninsula Academy; cooking classes taught by the hotel's chefs. This is a city seething with shops, but you could elect to just stay within the Peninsula Arcade; it has 100 shops under the one roof. High-end labels include Prada, Louis Vuitton, Versace, Cartier, Manolo Blahnik and the local-gone-global Shanghai Tang; many specialty stores too, from opticians to arts, crafts and antiques. The Peninsula Boutique has take-home gifts of its special teas, chocolates and secret recipe XO sauce.

The Long Bar at Felix

Outside, there are multiple-choice attractions in this hectic city. Visit the flower and bird markets, the Magic Kingdom of Disneyland; day trip into mainland China, take the Star Ferry to Central and Aberdeen Harbour to the giant Jumbo Floating Restaurant or hydrofoil across to Macau. Just over the road are the Space Museum and the Avenue of Stars (stars of stage and screen, that is). A bronze Bruce Lee is the leading light.

When you return from your excursion, glad to be back in this venerable hotel, as immaculate as its lovely old car, you might like to consider this fact. The Peninsula's team of pageboys open the large double glass doors about 4,000 times a day.

A bronze Bruce Lee

Jumbo Floating Restaurant

The Peninsula Hong Kong
Kowloon
China

Tel: (852) 2920 2888
Fax: (852) 2722 4170
E-mail: phk@peninsula.com
Internet: hongkong.peninsula.com

The ornate façade of
the Grand Hotel Europa

Check in, Check out ...

Grand Hotel Europa / Prague, Czech Republic

Since the collapse of the Iron Curtain, and the Velvet Revolution that led to the fall of the Communist government, Prague has been a popular travel destination on the European circuit. One of its main attractions is the exquisite core of 18th-century Baroque buildings that preserve the spirit of the Hapsburg Empire in the 18th and 19th centuries.

There is ample evidence that Prague is going global; transnational labels such as Marks & Spencer and Benetton, and the ubiquitous American hamburger are some of the clues that capitalism is effecting changes. But the city is full of signs to other times and cultures. Prague's most familiar monument is the medieval Charles Bridge, a pedestrian promenade for 600 years, and home to souvenir sellers and artists. It spans the River Vltava, between the Mala Strana (Little Quarter) and the Old Town, and nearby is the Prague Castle. The buildings enclosed within the castle walls include a palace, churches, art gallery, the writer Franz Kafka's house and a monastery.

The lobby entrance

The ground floor café

Mozart lived here while composing his opera *Don Giovanni*, and the piano he composed it at is displayed in the Mozart Museum. The Estates Theatre is where the opera was premiered in 1787. The Old Town Square is still the heart of Prague, and the winding cobbled streets and medieval arcades of the Old Town evoke the mysterious and dark world of the past. This is another city for wandering around, it is easy and intriguing to walk through, or alternatively to take a tram.

Wenceslas Square is home to many of Prague's Art Nouveau buildings. The Grand Hotel Europa is one of the more spectacular examples. Its statue-topped façade is painted and wrapped with hand-sculpted wrought-iron railings, and lettered in faded old gold. Seats on the ground floor café's outdoor terrace are in demand for style and people watching but not for food or service, not the strong suit of this hotel. The first floor café is grandly fitted with chandeliers and hand-carved wood, but the service is as variable as the weather. The best rooms are the large and high ceilinged front-facing doubles. Some have balconies overlooking the square, the site of riots and revolutions in 1448, 1968 and 1989.

A hard to find example of modern Prague architecture is the Ginger and Fred Building, by Frank Gehry, one building that has two different parts, as did the famous dancing duo of Hollywood films. Apparently located on Rasinovo Nabrezi, this Gehry landmark could not, or would not, be found by the taxi driver. It was tempting to crown him with more than the Czech coins.

A front-facing room

Grand Hotel Europa
Prague
Czech Republic

Tel: (420 2) 2421 5387
Fax: (420 2) 2422 4544
E-mail: info@evropahotel.cz
Internet: www.evropahotel.cz

Rendezvous

L'Hotel . / Paris, France

The concept of romance and the city of Paris are closely connected. City of light, city of love; long regarded as somewhere to have a love affair in and to be always in love with, in the springtime, or anytime, as the song goes.

Simply named, easy to remember in any language, L'Hotel has a history of intrigue; it was an 18th-century *pavilion d'amour*. Purpose-built as a place for trysts, this romantic rendezvous is a *bijou* hotel – a jewel nestled in the very heart of Paris. It certainly feels like being in a jewelry box inside the little blue velvet-quilted lift that only takes two – and a very small valise. The ambiance and design is *belle époque*, with all the embellishments of another era. This is a liaison between décor and decadence; with swags of plush curtains, rich velvets on antique furniture, ornately painted and intricately carved ceilings, dramatic patterned wallpapers, dark colours and gold highlights.

Although it is architecturally beautiful inside, the hotel has a rather plain façade. Its address is marked out with a plaque recalling perhaps its most famous guest, dramatist Oscar Wilde. This is where he died, in 1900. His brilliant literary career ended in scandal, prison and exile, but his compositions and epigrams persist.

Le Bélier restaurant and patio.

Lobby of L'Hotel

You may find yourself
in a room reminiscent
of **antique Japan**,
the Arabian Nights
or Africa.

Oscar Wilde's last words were about a decorative issue. "My wallpaper and I are fighting a duel to the death. One or other of us has to go". The wallpaper won. That pattern has long gone, but befitting the dandy he was, there is now a brilliant emerald green peacock fresco on two of the walls in what was once his room. Like a stage-set from one of his plays, its Victorian decor partly recreates his London dining room.

The rooms are circled around the magnificent oval atrium, which rises six floors to a sky-lit glass dome. L'Hotel's bedrooms are all in character, though not the same one. They mix times, personalities and place. Behind each door is a different style. You may find yourself in a room reminiscent of baroque Italy; antique Japan: the Arabian Nights or Africa. Others are in neo-Gothic or Art Deco style, patterned with leopard-skin or coloured in Cardinal scarlet. Or you can sleep amongst the many mirrors and memorabilia of French stage star Mistinguett. All are ornately detailed, two have terraces that look out over the roofs of Saint Germain des Prés. Down in the stone vaults of the hotel and reminiscent of a Roman bath, there is a hammam and swimming pool; rare in old Paris hotels, and a godsend during a sweltering summer.

L' Hotel has one of the best locations on the Left Bank: in walking distance of the Louvre, Musée D'Orsay and Nôtre Dame, in the midst of art galleries, antique stores, fashion boutiques, famous cafés and restaurants.

Bedroom of Room 16 – Oscar Wilde Suite

The atrium

In 1989, the glass and steel pyramid designed by I.M.Pei settled like some transparent alien ship landing in the courtyard of the Louvre Museum. Many were disapproving of it, but most are now accepting of its practical benefit and different beauty. Before it was built, the concept set off similar arguments to those raised when the Eiffel Tower was first proposed: a resistance to the imposition of a radical new structure on a historic and treasured site. Now the pyramid is judged a Paris landmark.

Cohabiting and coexisting with its august host, it functions as a brilliant new visitor entrance to the Louvre, an elegant connection to the galleries below the courtyards. Asked why he chose a pyramid shape, its architect

The underground swimming pool

replied that "formally, it is the most compatible with the architecture of the Louvre; it is also one of the most structurally stable of forms, which assures its transparency, and as it is constructed of glass and steel, it signifies a break with the architectural traditions of the past."

For readers of Dan Brown's blockbuster novel *The Da Vinci Code*, it has another significance. If you haven't read the book yet, skip the next sentence. This is where the hero follows the clues to discover the secret burial spot of the Holy Grail. You can locate another real place of note here; Café Marly, opening onto a stone terrace beside the Louvre. Over coffee you can survey the pyramid and then stroll back to the baroque charm of L'Hotel, just minutes away.

L'Hotel
Paris
France
Tel: (33 1) 44 41 99 00
Fax: (33 1) 43 25 64 81
E-mail: reservation@l-hotel.com
Internet: www.l-hotel.com

Fortress France

Château de Bagnols does not fit the fairy-tale version of a traditional wedding-cake style castle. This is a fortress to be taken seriously, a vantage point built in the early 13th century to forewarn defenders of approaching enemies.

Conceived in the age of chivalry, the fortress may have a new vocation as a hotel, but it upholds the medieval tradition of hospitality toward visitors. Guests are welcomed through its portcullis, their transport tethered and tended to in the parking areas, rather than the former stables, converted as part of the accommodation adjoining the Château.

With towers, moat and a drawbridge entrance, the Château de Bagnols is a triumph of restoration over ruin. Originally built in 1221, it is now one of the historic treasures of France. But it was left to molder after the Revolution, and a decade ago it was a sadly neglected ruin, with leaking roofs, cracked walls, a home to a family of crows and surrounded by a wilderness garden.

Prince Charming may have come late but the fortress has been awakened from its long sleep to again become the great property it once was.

Traces of the avenues and bassins marking the axis of the old garden were uncovered in the overgrown orchard, enclosed by a stone wall punctuated with small round decorative towers. An avenue of limes follows the terrace walls and four parterres, planted with cherry trees, are sheltered by yew hedges. The restored grounds recreate the original gardens, which, like the Château, overlook the little medieval village of Bagnols and the hills beyond.

View of the Château from the garden

The entrance, with the courtyard beyond

A contemporary touch is the glass wall that allows a view of the sleek courtyard kitchen where regional specialties are prepared. The Beaujolais style of cuisine has been described by Elizabeth David as "the most sumptuous kind of country cooking brought to a point of finesse, beyond which it would lose its character."

Many meet for coffee or aperitifs in the Grand Salon, where they are spoiled for viewing choice: splendid wall paintings or large windows offering views over the countryside and into the courtyard. When we visited, the room was decorated with massive bowls of peony roses, out of season at that time of the year. The elaborately carved Renaissance fireplace dominates the room, and at each side of the hearth, doors lead to tower rooms.

Staying here is well worth the expense, and the privacy and shelter found behind the castle walls have appealed to many wearied by fame. The Château is peaceful and perfect without being pretentious. Sitting on the terrace looking out over the gardens to the hills and valleys beyond is to be lord of all you survey, which one guest, Charles VIII of France, assuredly was. The King's visit in 1490 is commemorated by the royal coat of arms above the dining room's Gothic fireplace.

The hotel's 20 rooms and suites have been expertly restored and each has a different character. Antique beds are hung with period silk velvets and embroideries, and dressed with pure linen embroidered sheets fit for modern-day royalty.

Preserved within the Château's massive walls are a series of striking wall paintings, examples of embellishments added in times of peace and prosperity. The earliest date from the 15th century. Many were hidden behind partitions, plasterwork and other modifications made over time, and were only discovered during recent restoration work.

The Château exudes history and grandeur, but these qualities never overwhelm the aura of comfort and sense of human scale. Its bucolic setting, the Beaujolais region in the east of France, has been compared with Tuscany. This, though, is quieter and less visited. Rolling green hills are blanketed with forest and vineyard, and hilltop villages, picturesque châteaux, fine churches and farm buildings are constructed of the local honey-colored stone known as *pierre dorée* (golden stone).

The Grand Salon with its
Renaissance fireplace

The bedroom of the Guichard D'Oingt suite

In the weeks of autumn, the vine leaves turn color and the grape harvest is brought in at the famous vineyards that make up the Beaujolais wine trail. The fruit is picked by hand in the vineyards such as Fleurie, Julienas and St-Amour; and the wines are drunk – with others produced by neighboring Burgundy and Rhône – at the Château and restaurants in the surrounding towns which include St-Paule and Villefranche.

A headstart on decorating a more modest castle can be made in the Château's boutique shop, where customers may be tempted by a collection of more than 500 specially designed items. This stock includes handblown French glasses inspired by an 18th-century Burgundian design, furniture, silverware and Limoges porcelain. The charming pink and white uniforms of the housemaids are not for sale.

The Château is open from April to January, and would provide a great retreat for Christmas. Arrangements can be made with the management to open during the closed season, should you wish to have a castle to yourself.

The Beaujolais countryside viewed from the terrace

Château de Bagnols

Bagnols-en-Beaujolais
France

Tel: (33 474) 714 000
Fax: (33 474) 714 049
E-mail: alain.ravier@wanadoo.fr
Internet: www.bagnols.com

An old cart from bygone Bagnols days

Land of Plenty

Hôtel Cuq en Terrasses / Cuq-Toulza, France

To grow well, sunflowers need full sun. Basking in the midsummer warmth, rows and rows of vibrant sunflowers are standing in their fields, bright battalions massed at the sides of the road as we drive past. Some of them are standing straight, heads held up high, others seem to be leaning over slightly as if they are still asleep, but all are facing the same direction: east, like pilgrims at prayer.

Sun worship is their religion. In a field of blooming sunflowers most flowerheads are turned toward the east, where the sun rises each morning. Yet when the plant is still in bud, it actually follows the movement of the sun across the horizon as it moves from east to west.

This tracking motion is driven by motor cells in a flexible segment of the stem just below the bud. When the blooming stage is reached that stem locks, so that once the flower opens into vivid yellow petals it faces east for the rest of its short but colorful life.

In French, their name is *tournesol*; and the translation is a literal one – it means "turn with the sun." Spread out like a quilt of ocher and green, sunflowers are a symbol of the radiant light here in the Lauragais, in the southwest of France. Sun seekers in the know track here, from all points of the compass, turning to the warmth and comfort of the Hôtel Cuq en Terrasses.

The hotel

As many dream of doing,
they left the city and moved to the
country, when they discovered
this special part of it to live in.

Once a presbytery, the 18th-century building is now rejuvenated as a truly charming hilltop hotel in the hamlet of Cuq le Château in the region of Cuq-Toulza. It is well positioned in the heart of the ancient Pays de Cocagne, now the region of Tarn; in the center of a triangle formed by the cities and towns of Toulouse, Carcassonne and Albi, and close to several of the loveliest villages in France. Simple and well-restored, the old house is much larger than it looks from its front entrance on the main street of what is almost like a film set of a tiny time-has-stood-still-here French village. The backdrop from one window in the library–living room is the village church; at the other end of

The terrace

the room the scene is of golden fields, green valleys and distant blue hills. Once you have arrived, you will either go upstairs to your room, or downstairs, then walk down further, to the dining room and out on to the wide terracotta-tiled terrace: the heart of the hotel. From here, there are still more layers in this multileveled location: of gardens shaded by spreading mulberry trees, down to the swimming pool, and nearby a separate and secluded Tower suite. The bedrooms are all handsomely designed and outfitted in traditional *midi* style. None are alike, so you can return here at least seven times before you will have stayed in them all.

The salon and library

Dinner is on request here, but it seems to be more in demand; such is the reputation and standard of the cooking that when they have had a taste of it guests make sure they are in for the evening. Chef Andonis Vassalos creates the food, bringing extra flavors to the French cuisine from his native Greece, while partner Philippe Gallice complements the menu from the wine cellar. As many dream of doing, they left the city and moved to the country, when they discovered this special part of it to live in. Sitting out on the terrace, savoring a glass of velvety red or crisp cool white in the late afternoon sun, delicious aromas in the air as dinner is being prepared, you will start to fantasize making your own escape to somewhere as idyllic. That's when most people decide to book here again.

La Lauragais bedroom

Yellow is a predominant color in this golden landscape, and blue is part of it too, woven into its history. Pays de Cocagne was the early name give to this area, when it was discovered that a rich blue pigment – *cocagne*, or "woad" – could be extracted from a local plant. It became a very valuable commodity much in demand for fabrics and art, and the region prospered.

Many intriguing destinations are within easy driving distance of the hotel. One is the city of Albi; at its center, the 15th-century St-Cécile Cathedral. This fortress cathedral is a masterpiece of Southern Gothic architecture and the largest brick building in the world.

But its most amazing feature is only on view from the inside. Painted with blue pastel by Italian painters from Bologna in 1509-1512, the frescoes on the cathedral's arched ceiling form the largest work of Italian Renaissance painting to be found anywhere in France. It is a visual biblical encyclopedia, an evocation of heaven played out on a blue and gold background, and just as they were when painted over five centuries ago. They have never been restored, their colors still vivid and lustrous in the low light. The spectacular scale, nearly 330 feet (100 m) long by 92 feet (28 m) wide, and the magnificence of the work makes it one of the most memorable sights of my life. A gigantic and graphic mural of the Last Judgement surrounds the church altar, no doubt as a reminder to the congregation of what could lie ahead.

Terre Cuite bedroom

The frescoed ceiling in St-Cécile Cathedral, Albi

Rich in history and scenery, as well as its many other food and wine assets, the region has also been described as a "Land of Plenty, a smiling country," where everything is found in abundance; bright yellow fields of sunflowers, groves of oak trees, checkered hues of cultivated fields, warm clear light and friendly people. You can see and experience all of this, and turn your head to follow the sun, relaxing at the Hotel Cuq en Terrasses. Three stars is its *appellation*, but its surroundings make it more.

Hotel Cuq en Terrasses
Cuq-Toulza
France

Tel: (33 563) 825 400
Fax: (33 563) 825 411
E-mail: info@cuqenterrasses.com
Internet: www.cuqenterrasses.com

Moonstruck

Anchored just offshore from the near-mythical South Pacific island of Bora Bora, is "The Motu" – a special retreat on an island set apart. In Polynesian legend, Bora Bora is a sacred island, the first to rise out of the sea. Protected by a barrier reef and its blue crystalline lagoon, it is surrounded by a myriad of small motus – islets. It's from this that "The Motu" takes its simple name.

The eternal lure of islands has drawn travelers in search of peace, quiet and isolation – or at least the illusion of it – to tropical arcadia such as this, from time immemorial. The soothing sound of waves lapping on the shore, or crashing on the distant reef, often lulls the stressed into a blissful state of relaxation and sleep. A stunning climate, spectacular scenery and beautiful beaches – for sunning on by day and strolls afterdinner in the moonlight – are on the wish list of island-holiday seekers.

Fishing nets drying

Hand in hand,
on the edge of the sand,
**they danced by the light
of the moon.**
Edward Lear

Searching for a place to stay in Bora Bora, we saw an artist's sketch of a new hotel in progress. Our inquiring fax drew this descriptive e-mail response.

Dear Shelley-Maree, ia orana (hello)!

My name is Frédéric Lemoine-Romain, I'm the assistant of Denis de Schrevel (General Manager), we are both in charge of the two Sofitels of Bora Bora (Sofitel Coralia Marara & Sofitel Coralia Motu). As Denis is out of the island, I'm answering now to your fax. I can give you some of the following informations to help you :

• the Motu is a private and exclusive resort; with 20 deep overwater and 10 deluxe (built on the island) bungalows (total 30), around 60 persons max. living on this property

• the environnement of the Motu is really exceptionnal (natural coral gardens, small hill with tremendous and amazing vues (several all around), different plants, ambiance climate depending where you are on the island, facing the famous Otemanu mountain of Bora Bora (in the best angle vue), area of reproduction of the famous heron (protected or preserved area for us, this is also the logo of the Motu) ...

• for all those reasons we decided to developpe a specific concept to offer to our guests of the Motu :

1. Luxury and Sauvage

2. Simplicity and Authenticity

The Motu – island in the sun

The frangipane flower

View from the Motu of Bora Bora's twin peaks

- Luxury: inside of each bungalow and in the communal area (materials used, furnitures ...)

- Sauvage: outside of the bungalow considering the beauty of the nature (sea, lagoon, the island in itself, protection of the environnement, back to the nature for each guest, in a large majority coming from cities ...)

- Simplicity: human size island (one-hour walking round trip), where the communal area is the heart, for simplicity and comfort (welcome area, activities desk, lounge bar, restaurant in the same "grand salon," panoramic one, closed from each bungalow ...)

- Authenticity: in a real Tahitian ambiance (local staff from BOB), with local roofs, kohu wood used worked by Tahitian people knowing this wood very well, some of the employees able to give a real traditional and authentic touch for the guests that looked for it (barbecue on the island, explanations of tradition ...)

- As it stays a small hotel, we can imagine offering to those exclusive guests something more than a hotel: like personalization of all the different services guests of the Motu, for us, exclusive guests, will have a direct boat transfer from the airport to the Motu (if possible, checkin in the boat). This exclusive resort is not built to

Overwater bungalow 121

accept children and please no noise for our exclusive guests. Overwater and deluxe have the same space (49 m² inside + terasse), but overwater have add in each a round glass floor for the vue, and a large sundeck (12 m²) with outside shower + steps and ladder to go in the water. Deluxe bungalow, very deep overwater with sundeck open to the lagoon. Three beaches, sunny, several spots to use in the nature for picnic, relaxing small local "fare," outside barbecue … – As it is an upscale, private, and specific place, we added a permanent coordinator in charge of the stays of the guests, for a real personalization and quality.

I really hope that this e-mail will help you to confirm to yourself, that we could probably be in your next edition, as soon as you will visiting us, you'll be, I'm sure!!!

Please receive our tropical and sincere best regards.

Frédéric Lemoine-Romain

Executive Assistant Manager

Bathroom of 121

Boats at anchor in the lagoon

Sometimes a man hits upon
a place to which
**he mysteriously feels
that he belongs.**
W. Somerset Maugham

We started packing immediately. And here you can see for yourself much of what Frederic described so well. For those who seek a temporary escape, this is an ideal runaway destination. The high cost of living the South Seas' dream here is a price worth paying for something to remember long after you return to the real world.

The Motu at sunset

The Sofitel Coralia Motu
Bora Bora
French Polynesia
Tel: (689) 67 70 46
Fax: (689) 67 74 03
E-mail: h8989@accor-hotels.com

Eau de Cologne

Cologne, Germany

You certainly can't miss this hotel, the tallest building by far in the neighborhood. The former water reservoir, once Europe's largest, has been transformed into a contemporary and intriguing hotel.

The water tower was built between 1868 and 1872 by an English engineer, but it was made obsolete by an underground watermain system laid in the early 1900s. During World War II the lower floors of the water tower served as an air-raid shelter, but the upper floors were partially destroyed.

In the 1980s, plans were conceived to convert the neglected building into a hotel. After four years of reconstruction work, including the rebuilding of the top floors and inserting windows in the blind arches, the Hotel in Watertower opened to guests in 1990.

The architectural monument is a bricklayer's heaven, with old and new brickwork a major feature of the interior, particularly in the reception. Thirty-six feet (11 m) high brick pillars with steel connecting bridges suspended across the core of the tower accentuate the interior's feeling of height and optical illusion. Furnishings were chosen by French designer Andrée Putman, an appropriate choice for this ultimate recycling project since she has expressed a belief in design being redemptive and a goal of creating things that last.

For the tower's new vocation as a hotel, she has used a cylindrical theme for many of the furnishings – armchairs, wall lamps, side tables, carpets and door handles appear as whole or halved cylinders.

Counterpointing the rich brown of the bricks are dark wenge wood, and a palette of vanilla and sand tones, with rich yellow and royal blue used on velvet-covered furniture reminiscent of Art Deco.

The Hotel im Wasserturm in its park-like surroundings

The reception desks in the hotel lobby are an amusing play on the round theme, with the two halves forming a mirror image, an unusual effect for the arriving and departing guest. Time whiled away in the bar, also semi-circular, can induce confusion as you amble back to your room, when one side of the hotel is the same as the other. In this case, seeing double is not always a result of drinking too much. But even the strictly sober may not want to look down as they walk across metal bridging to their rooms.

The two halves of one circle reception

The view from the rooftop terrace circling the restaurant is spectacular, taking in the medieval and modern city of Cologne, its trademark twin-towered cathedral, and the river Rhine. The restaurant interior seems somewhat at odds with the rest of the hotel design, but the food is excellent and the vista no less so. On a clear day this is an ideal vantagepoint for a visual tour of the city.

The Wasserturm's location makes for quiet surroundings more typical of a country hotel than one close to the center of a major European city. It is a handy refuge for anyone exhibiting or visiting the myriad of trade fairs hosted by Cologne, which range from fashion to photography to food.

If you prefer to stay sequestered in the tower, choose one of the studio rooms, which feel more like apartments. Whitewashed and spacious, they have great curved windows, screened to soften and diffuse the light.

The other imposing structure on the skyline is the Gothic Cathedral, which was begun in 1248 and completed in 1880. It attracts visitors and pilgrims to see its golden shrine of the Magi. The cathedral's distinctive spires are an enduring symbol of a city with many Romanesque churches. Other attractions are shopping in the Old Town, sailing on the Rhine River or visiting museums. The great variety of museums include one with Europe's largest collection of American Pop Art, a Beatles museum and the taste-sensational Museum of Chocolate.

Living room of studio bedroom

Curved lines in the bathroom

At the Imhoff-Stollwerck-Museum – which is itself an interesting building on a peninsular jutting out into the Rhine – there is the opportunity to explore the history and culture of chocolate. "Light is shed on the dark past of this brown delicacy!" With a tropical hothouse that is full of cocoa trees and exotic plants; a working chocolate factory where visitors can see how chocolate bars, truffles and hollow Easter bunnies are made, and a fountain that is actually flowing with hot chocolate, this museum is a real must to visit, smell and taste. And yes, there is a museum shop as well, in addition to a river terrace restaurant to rest up at if all that cacao has gone to your head!

The bronze Wasserturm room key, a miniature version of the Watertower, is far too heavy to forget to leave at reception.

The room key,
hotel in miniature

Hotel im Wasserturm
Koln
Germany
Tel: (49 221) 200 80
Fax: (49 221) 200 88 88
E-mail: info@hotel-im-wasserturm.de
Internet: www.hotel-im-wasserturm.de

London Pride

| The Halkin Hotel | London, Great Britain |

A little perennial plant, London Pride is symbolic of the enduring spirit of London, a city that survived the Great Fire of 1666, and the bombing Blitz of World War II. One of the great cultural melting-pot cities of the world, London absorbs and transforms those who arrive from other countries. Now home to almost every race and religion, this vast city attracts a constant wave of visitors.

Britain's pomp and pageantry, a formalized show business that is associated with an aristocracy headed by the Royals, continues to be one of London's major tourist attractions. Ceremonies like the Changing of the Guard at Buckingham Palace and the annual Trooping the Colour are rituals and symbols of an enduring, albeit dented, monarchy.

The Halkin Hotel

Room 506

London reeks of history. Small blue plaques affixed to many of its buildings commemorate the famous and the infamous, both real and invented, who lived in them; every step is where someone celebrated has gone before – from Charles Dickens to Sherlock Holmes. This is a metropolis with a very long and mixed record. The source and inspiration of much great writing and art, it is also home to a raft of museums and galleries. It seems that the city is itself a museum and full of them, from the eccentric Sir John Soane's House to the Victoria & Albert and the British Museum.

Green spaces are essential to relieve the urban crush. Hyde Park and St. James Park are two that fulfil a function as "the lungs of London." Not far from either park, in the heart of Belgravia, is the Halkin Hotel. Sister to – perhaps the more elegant older sister – the much promoted and "hip" Metropolitan Hotel, the Halkin is stylish in a discreet manner, modern but not of the moment. Its polished design is more for the long run. The traditional Neo-Renaissance exterior belies its modern Italian-designed interior, which is sleek and contemporary, yet elegant and comfortable.

Each floor of the hotel has been named after and themed on a color associated with a different element: water, air, fire, earth and sky. The fusion of Italy and the Orient (its owner, Christina Ong, is Singaporean) is evident in its design style. Subtle feng shui references are in the curves and circles used throughout the hotel.

A predominantly black and ivory interior has warmth added to it by rich wood veneers, and arched windows that let in the often bright London light. The hotel is favored by fashion people, who will approve the staff clad in Armani uniforms and appreciate the black accents in the spacious rooms. The deep baths in the big marble bathrooms are perfect for a luxurious soak after a hard day of sight-seeing or business meetings. But just what you need to prepare yourself for an outstanding meal in the hotel's Michelin-starred Italian restaurant overlooking a lush green private garden, a characteristic feature of London's inner elite areas.

When a man is tired of London, he is tired of life; **for there is in London all that life can afford.**
Samuel Johnson

Bathroom of 506

The lobby

Discreetly located – knowledgeable London taxi drivers will know it's off
Grosvenor Place – in a quiet street, the Halkin is within walking distance
of the shopping mecca of Knightsbridge, home to a host of name stores,
streets and convenient for the museums of South Kensington. (The
automatic spellchecker on my computer suggests the correct spelling of
the hotel's name should be Halcyon; it certainly has that atmosphere.)

The Halkin Hotel
London
Great Britain
Tel: (44 207) 333 1058
Fax: (44 207) 333 1100
E-mail: res@halkin.co.uk

The view from Hotel Tresanton

Coasting

St. Mawes, Great Britain

The Roseland Peninsula is on the warmer, calmer, southern side of Cornwall, a region that has extreme weather and rugged terrain, yet can be one of the mildest places in mainland Britain.

The Hotel Tresanton is moored here, once a yacht club, and then a hotel for yachtsmen, it is now owned, restored and reopened in its new rigging by Olga Polizzi, the sister of Rocco Forte. All the rooms, as well as the hotel terrace, have stunning sea views, looking out across the harbor to the St. Anthony lighthouse. "Tresanton" means the road to St. Anthony, and en route by car you must pass through St. Mawes. This is a seaside fishing village such as you might expect to see in a film, a movie-set creation of a picture-postcard example that still seems undiscovered and unspoiled despite the summer-season crowds. Of course those who live and visit here have discovered it already. But in winter it can seem magically empty and atmospheric.

Hotel Tresanton is at the edge of the town, at the Castle end, a cluster of old houses on different levels built up the hill. It is blessed with a bewitching outlook, which could easily distract from the inner aspects. This is a hotel richly furnished yet simply fitted, with an attention to detail that reveals itself on close inspection. A sure hand has put this hotel together and made its interior prospect very pleasing to the eye.

Hotel Tresanton

This is a hotel with the atmosphere of a home, the lines between the two becoming blurred in an age of concern for and devotion to comfort. The Tresanton feels as though it is a private country house by the sea that takes in guests. Its large, comfortable sitting room reflects the character of its owners with a collection of furniture that seems to have evolved as it does at home, rather than having all arrived at once ready for opening day. A pleasing mix of old and new, there are plenty of plush settees and chairs to choose from if you have to share the room with others.

Each of the guestrooms is furnished differently with antiques and eclectic pieces, and all have a similar big view. The colors are soothing seaside-appropriate combinations, but fresh takes on that classic theme. Quietly luxurious, detail is understated but not overlooked in the deceptively simple rooms. There is space to move leisurely about, and in keeping with the coastal setting, the rooms are filled with the clear Cornish light.

The Tresanton has its own small cinema, an indulgence that seems preferable in every way to many other possible hotel offerings, such as fitness centers. Except that the cinema is only for use on rainy days – presumably there are some, as there are racks of rubber boots and umbrellas ready for such an event – and even these are attractively displayed.

A hotel by the sea should have a boat – here there is a fleet, from motorboats to a 48-foot classic racing yacht, the *Pinuccia*. Built to race for Italy in the 1939 World Cup, it is one of the sleekest and most timeless designs. Guests may charter the *Pinuccia*, with picnic and crew, to sail around the harbor.

Dinner in the restaurant, with the chef that has been lured from London, where he trained with Marco Pierre White and the Roux brothers, gives the lie to any lingering doubts about provincial English cooking.

The sitting room

The entrance to the restaurant

Bathroom with mosaic floor

Now, nature, as I am only
too well aware, has
her enthusiasts, but on the whole,
I am not to be counted among
them. To put it rather bluntly,
I am not the type who
wants to go back to the land;
I am the type who wants
to go back to the hotel.
Fran Leibowitz

St. Mawes Castle, built by Henry VIII in response to the Pope's threat to send a crusade against dissenting England, is just up the road. Behind and beside the hotel a beautiful little garden with a rare collection of subtropical and Mediterranean plants grows happily in this benign climate. A variety of other expeditions beckon further afield, such as to the Lost Gardens of Heligan – lost no more, but the Found Gardens is less poetic – or to the Tate Gallery in St. Ives.

With a cup of good coffee and a book, I was content to watch the sea and the land from my chair on the terrace. Surveying one of the greatest views in England, I felt as though I was on the upper deck, on the bridge of my own ship, and that a life on the ocean wave was the life for me. The restorative sea air is one very good reason to go south.

Seaside bedroom

View of St. Mawes from the Tresanton's terrace

Hotel Tresanton
Cornwall
Great Britain

Tel: (44 132) 627-0055
Fax: (44 132) 627-0053
E-mail: info@tresanton.com
Internet: www.tresanton.com

Ornamentation

Mandeville Hotel London, Great Britain

A medieval English knight, Sir John Mandeville, was once the most famous travel writer in Europe. He went on a pilgrimage to Jerusalem in 1322, and did not return home until 34 years later. The publication of *The Travels of Sir John Mandeville* was a sensation in the 14th century. Claiming to have visited India, China, Java and Sumatra, he declared that his journey proved that it was possible to sail around the world. His tales significantly influenced generations of Renaissance explorers; Christopher Columbus read his book before setting out in search of the Americas. Shakespeare, Swift, Defoe and Coleridge were just some of the many writers inspired by his stories. However, by the 19th century, critical scholars slated Mandeville. He was thought to have been a tall-tale teller, perhaps a fraud. The wanderer who fascinated his readers by writing that in the Indian Ocean "there is a race of great stature, like giants ... they have one eye only, in the middle of their foreheads" quite likely embellished his adventures.

Behind the plain Victorian façade of the hotel *not* named after him, embellishment is used to great effect. The eclectic interior of the Mandeville Hotel combines baroque ornamentation with modernist furniture, spiced with witty theatrical details.

The deVigne Bar

Arriving at the Mandeville

Top: An alcove in the deVille Restaurant
Below: The deVigne Bar

The return of vintage patterns is welcome after ages of minimalism. Given a contemporary update with color and scale, they add vitality to the sophisticated bar and restaurant. Glass chandeliers in 60s' style illuminate modern and antiqued furnishings, and a fresh palette of white, Weimaraner brown – a precise description of the color also known as taupe – and silver adds light and elegance to the dining room. Afternoon tea – designer cupcakes and sensible scones – is served here, on pink china designed by fashion icon Zandra Rhodes, with pink tea or pink champagne.

At night, inventive lighting makes the atmosphere more theatrical. At first glance the portraits in the bar appear to be traditional Elizabethan; a closer look reveals lips enhanced with vivid lipstick.

Most of the bedroom suites, perhaps appropriately, are less exuberant in their design than the rest of the hotel, albeit stylish. The loftiest is the penthouse, its terrace overlooking city rooftops.

Reception

The Penthouse Suite

Top: The London Eye
Below: The towers of London – old and new

For 21st century explorers, the Mandeville is ideally located, just off Oxford Street, a few minutes walk to Marylebone Village, Mayfair and Regent's Park. Quintessential London stores like Selfridges, Liberty and Conran are quite literally across the road or around the corner. Art auction houses Sotheby's and Christies, and the investigative Sherlock Holmes Museum are nearby. A diverse array of bars and restaurants are on the doorstep too, many with outdoor seating, ideal for people-watching on London's often sultry summer nights.

The blend of old and new in the Mandeville is typical of this eminent city. Contemporary and medieval architecture co-exist in a culturally diverse metropolis, much embellished over the ages.

Mandeville Hotel
London
Great Britain

Tel: (44 207) 935-5599
Fax: (44 207) 935-9588
E-mail: info@mandeville.co.uk
Internet: www.mandeville.co.uk

Cliffhanger

Perivolas Traditional Houses | Oia-Santorini, Greece

Clinging to vertiginous volcanic rock cliffs high above the caldera is the village of Oia. The brilliant Aegean sun strikes its white roofs and blue domes, lighting a picture-postcard view of the dramatic landscape.

Santorini is the southernmost island of the Greek Cyclades. Thousands of visitors, in the summer especially, flood here to visit this spectacular island, which legend suggests is home to the drowned ancient city of Atlantis.

Born of a volcano in prehistoric times, Santorini's ancient slopes were fractured by an immense eruption into multicolored cliffs, black and ocher and tan, nearly a thousand feet high. Where there once was a mountain peak is now a caldera, the deep cavity in the summit of the extinct volcano, forming a cauldron for the sea. In the cliff face, sheltered from the strong north wind, people dug skafta, small rooms with barrel-vaulted ceilings. Earthquakes regularly shook the tiny villages, life was hard, and many left for Athens or the New Worlds of America and the Antipodes. In 1956 there were devastating earthquakes. One positive aftermath was that roads were built, and electricity installed. A new industry of tourism began. Now many ships cross the harbor, aircraft fly in daily and in the main town of Phira, cafés, shops and people crowd the streets. Discos and big hotels are down on the black sand beaches of Perissa and Kamari.

EUROPE + ASIA + NORTH AMERICA + SOUTH AMERICA + OCEANIA + AFRICA

On the northernmost tip of Santorini is the small picturesque town of
Oia, built high on the rim of the caldera. A winding stairway connects it
with the harbor far below, and its stepped paths lead through less crowded
but still busy streets. On the edge of Oia is Perivolas, 16 traditional houses,
skafta converted from old wineries and stables into perfectly situated places
to stay. The group of houses is family owned and strictly respects the
traditional local character. Restoration of the houses has been under the
supervision of a scholar of Santorinian architecture.

Perivolas Traditional Houses

Perivolas House 15

Each house is simply furnished in the Cycladic style, complemented with many antiques from all over the Aegean Islands. All are self-contained with spacious niches for beds, little kitchens, bathrooms with smoothed concrete floors, and hand-carved walls that are cool to the touch. Each is unique in its shape and character, and all have their own stone terrace. The houses step down to the bar and breakfast room, which opens onto a pool that curves over the edge of the cliff into the great panorama beyond.

The view is simply astounding, almost confrontational, a dazzling vista of bluest sky and sea with dark red cliffs beyond. Watching the changing colors of this dramatic landscape as the day begins, through to the spectacular sunset that ends it, is a pleasure free to all who have eyes to see it.

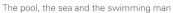

The pool, the sea and the swimming man

Oia architecture

The boundaries between the sea and the pool are blurred, a precipitous drop from the edge of one to the surface of the other. Houses and rock also blend together, and here on the terrace of this peaceful perch high above the caldera, with a glass or two of the crisp white Santorini wine, it is easy to forget that there is another world beyond.

Sunrise over Oia

Perivolas Traditional Houses

Oia-Santorini
Greece

Tel: (30 286) 607-1308
Fax: (30 286) 607-1309
E-mail: info@perivolas.gr
Internet: www.perivolas.gr

The Lake Palace Hotel

Star of India

The Lake Palace Hotel   Udaipur, India

It was here, to the heat, color and noise of India, that we came directly from the Ice Hotel, another white building set in a converse landscape and climate. While poles apart – one marble mirrored in a lake, the other ice frozen to the ground – there was still a striking similarity in their stand-alone positions and glittering physical presence.

A first visit to India is an assault on some timid Western senses, the crowds of people pressing so close a shock, the beggars pathetic and unsettling and the demented traffic alarming. Our transit through Mumbai affected our nervous dispositions so much that we arrived in this comparatively quiet corner of India with an overwhelming sense of relief. This was tempered by the knowledge that at the Lake Palace Hotel we would be isolated and cocooned from real India.

The hotel is set apart from that reality, and rightly or wrongly, we were glad to be within its calm and sheltering walls. But as we were to find out later in our journey, the real world is never far away. Viewed from the hotel's roof terrace, the romantic lakeside city of Udaipur in the Indian state of Rajasthan is both a beautiful and grand sight. The forts and battlements rear up behind the houses like cobras waiting to strike, but they stay still as their lake water reflection.

Tea in the Amrit Sagar Bar

In the distance, crowds of women in bright-colored saris come down to the shore to do their household washing, a sobering sight for one used to programming a machine to perform that function. Built on rock on a lake surrounded by hills in the mid-18th century, the Lake Palace is shaped from pure white marble, from the domed chattris (pavilions), filigreed screens and carved columns, to the bottom of the swimming pool. Once the palace of Maharana Jagat Singh III (who built it so he could leave home and do what he liked without his father interfering) it is now a hotel mounded like rococco cake icing on 4 acres of rock.

Udaipur viewed from the Roof Terrace

The hotel has seven suites fit for modern day Maharana and Maharani. All are splendid, some astounding, with stained-glass windows, intricate inlays and carved silver headboards. Handknotted Kashmiri carpets, original Mewer miniature paintings and rare antiques embellish the interiors of the hotel, making it a showplace for many of the Rajasthani arts and crafts. The guestrooms are much more demurely decorated than the suites and accordingly modestly priced in comparison. As only guests may come aboard the Lake Palace, there is ample space to enjoy the gardens and terraces.

In a hotel full of real beauty, the Jharokha café is likely the most lovely of the many public spaces. Here and in the restaurant, the food was simply delicious.

The Ajjan Niwas Suite

The Ajjan Niwas Suite

The scarlet Royal Barge was restored by the production team on location here for the James Bond film *Octopussy*, working with Udaipur craftsmen who remembered the Gangaur boat as it was many years before. This is one of a fleet of 12, but is by far the most spectacular. On special occasions and dinner cruises it is rowed grandly around the lake by the best-dressed oarsmen in the business, who row with a stern countenance that can be somewhat disconcerting given the armor they sport. As we sat in the mid-afternoon sun by the lily pond, lazily writing postcards to friends and family, before we were due to leave for the airport, word came that our flight to Mumbai had been cancelled. There was no other scheduled from Udaipur that day, and there was not likely to be one tomorrow. The polite but harassed man at the hotel travel desk was sympathetic to our concern that we would miss our connecting flight that night to our next destination but his gentle shrug was eloquent in its helplessness. Suddenly a brick wall appeared and there behind it was the real world again. Fellow guests, Americans with Indian antecedents, who were in the same predicament, approached us with a plan.

Gangaur Boatmen

Five hours later we were passengers in a mad midnight chariot race with seemingly no rules, no lights and no traffic police. Driving through the black-ink night of rural India, a darkness occasionally punctuated with roadside campfires, in an Hindustani rental car aimed by a driver seemingly possessed by speed demons, and a confrontational spirit that came to the forefront every time a truck loomed in front of the headlights, was an adventure we wished we were not in. (The length of this sentence is nothing compared to how long the trip seemed to take.) Night driving on Indian roads can be an exhilarating experience, akin to playing Russian roulette. However, we completed our truck derby trial and arrived shaken but not stirred at a distant airport to resume our expedition, out of India.

The Gangaur boat

Amused and emboldened by our adventurous departure, we have since determined to return to India, and to the Lake Palace Hotel. The old local saying, *"Pichola Ro Pani Pachho Gher Lave,"* meaning the waters of the Pichola lake will always call you back home is likely more a spell. Next time, we will have a less inflexible itinerary and make time to explore the many facets that make up India.

The Lake Palace Hotel
Udaipur
India
Tel: (91 294) 252-8800
Fax: (91 294) 252-8700
Internet: www.thw.com/tajlakepalace

The Clarence Hotel and the Grattan Bridge over the River Liffey

Suppose our rooms at the hotel
were beside each other
and any fooling went on ...
James Joyce, from *Ulysses*

The main entrance of the Clarence

Boomtown

The Clarence Hotel   Dublin, Ireland

These words, forming a pink lettered neon sign, were written across the top of the Clarence Hotel when I first visited Dublin in October of 1997. It was a temporary installation, part of the Dublin Literary Festival. Neon quotes appeared all over the city center, recalling the words of writers who have lived in and written about Dublin – Joyce, Shaw, Beckett, Swift, Wilde ... I wish these modern, poetic sign writings had been retained, as a unique tribute to the writers who shaped the literary heritage of this vital city. Jonathan Swift, the 18th-century author of *Gulliver's Travels*, would not recognize the new dynamic Dublin, which he once described as "the most disagreeable place in Europe." W.B. Yeats referred to his hometown as "blind and ignorant." Criticized roundly by most of the writers now lionized by the city they spurned, contemporary Dublin is a favored European weekend destination, the most visited city after Paris.

Like the French capital, it is a city for walking – to savor the architecture and rub shoulders with Dubliners. With a fine collection of low-rise 18th-century buildings, wide streets and intimate pubs, this is a city of human proportions. Molly Malone may be a fond memory, but traders and buskers still work the busy streets. The heart of a revitalized Eire, modern Dublin has more buzz than blarney. The Ireland of leprechauns and begorrahs, for so long part of the Irish myth, is not to be found here, although the brogue is still evident. The Clarence Hotel edges a maze of cobbled streets known as the Temple Bar district, the city's social hub. The building's solid stone frontage overlooks the River Liffey, situated on Dublin's "left bank," between the Grattan and Ha'penny Bridges.

From its beginnings as a railway hotel in 1852, the Clarence has projected architectural dignity, a quality it retained even at its most shabby in the 1970s. Generations of Guinness and whiskey drinkers have frequented its bars. Bought by Bono and The Edge, members of the Dublin-based rock group U2, the Clarence has been restored as a spacious and aristocratic-feeling small hotel. A pale background of oak, leather and stone sets off its Arts and Crafts style. Traditional and contemporary are cleverly combined, with a simplicity reminiscent of Shaker design. Hotel staff are dressed in sharp gray suits with just a hint of the cassock in the cut of their jackets.

The warm relaxing environment is underpinned by the use of rich color – crimson, royal blue, purple, gold and chocolate – never all combined in the one scheme. Colorful and covetable original artwork by Irish artist Guggi is on show throughout the hotel.

The Study projects the feel of a country house or a gentlemen's club. This is a comfortable place to settle into the leather chairs, read the newspapers and sip coffee (or something stronger) as the soft Irish light filters through the high windows.

The Reading Room Study

The stylish Octagon bar and especially the snug wood-paneled back bar tempt you to an Irish beer or whiskey, in that quintessential Irish establishment, the pub.

In the former ballroom, the Tea Room Restaurant offers a mouth-watering menu. Posted on the wall of the "back door" to the Clarence, in Temple Bar, this also attracts passersby in search of good food.

The Penthouse Suite with grand piano, bar, great sound system, private garden terrace and open-air hot tub is a place to feel like a visiting member of the rock aristocracy. It offers one of the best views of Dublin, across to the Wicklow mountains and Dublin Bay.

If you want to get out and about, it is a short stroll to Grafton Street shopping, galleries, theaters, cafés, restaurants, clubs and bars, both traditional and contemporary. An impressive collection of contemporary design is on display and for sale in the Irish Craft Centre, five minutes' walk from the hotel. The parks of Merrion Square and St. Stephen's Green are the city's "emerald islands." They are lovely even on "soft days" — an Irish euphemism for rainy weather.

A bedroom view

The "Celtic Tiger" can be heard as well as seen, with renovation and rebuilding underway throughout the city and new hotels, restaurants and bars opening at a rapid rate in response to the growing number of visitors and locals. Ireland's economic success is founded on benevolent tax laws for overseas investors and European Union money. The mood of confidence and the country's positive international profile have seen many ex-pats return to their homeland to share in its newfound pride.

When the sun goes down, this is a party town. Not much of the old Irish puritanism is here – Dublin has the youngest population in Ireland, and even the no-longer-young act it. The city stays up late. The huge number of pubs caters to virtually every musical taste from folk through to contemporary. Many weekend "riverdancers" who come to trip the light fantastic go home with a hangover they may not think so grand on Monday.

Visitors can retrace the steps of past Dublin writers on the Literary Pub Crawl, the best excuse for drinking and talking I've ever heard. Actors, not short of a well-crafted witty line themselves, guide the tours of pubs where many of the city's famous (and infamous) drank and claimed their inspiration. Soaking up "culture" while testing the local beverages is an appealing combination even now.

For somewhere much quieter, no talking or drinking allowed, the Library at Trinity College is a bibliophile's dream, with its timber-vaulted ceiling and rows of books. The university is also the guardian of the Book of Kells, the treasured ninth-century illuminated manuscript of the Gospels.

Dublin was the focal point of the struggle for and against home rule. The General Post Office still bears the scars of the violent 1916 Easter Uprising, and it remains the favorite starting point for demonstrations. Also the site of the 1921 Declaration of Independence, the post office is on O'Connell Street, a broad avenue on the north side of the River Liffey, now seen as the less gentrified "new" city.

The Clarence Hotel
Dublin
Ireland
Tel: (353 1) 670-9000
Fax: (353 1) 670-7800
Internet: www.theclarence.ie

Elevator detail

The Penthouse hot tub

Bay Watch

La Minervetta Maison Sorrento, Italy

Seated on the terrace at La Minervetta is like being at the theater, in the center of the Grand Circle.

At twilight, as the sun dims, the show begins. In the distance, across the deepening blue waters of the great bay is the backdrop, a sleeping Mount Vesuvius, the lights of Naples. Below, stage left, is a sheer drop to a miniature village on the edge of a little bay. It is as though you are looking down, now from the gods, on an unsuspecting Lilliputian life, watching a tiny tableau like a child's toy town. A community is going about its daily business. Fishing boats return, restaurant tables are set, sun beds on the sliver of beach and along the piers are folded away, lamps and candles are lit.

The scene below is like a film set, a designer recreation of a traditional Italy, but look closely and you will see the ubiquitous cell phone clamped to most ears. Ferries to Capri and Naples cross center-stage, as do cruise ships; super and simple yachts dawdle past. Church bells tolling the time every hour and half hour, scooter "chatter," music, boat motors and voices carrying on the night air as bars and cafés come alive make up the soundtrack.

Grand view across
the Bay of Naples

La Minervetta

Perched high on a rock face near the southern Italian town of Sorrento, above the old fishing village of Marina Grande, all of La Minervetta's rooms have a spectacular outlook. Even the kitchen has a panoramic view that could distract all but the most dedicated cook. There are visual treats inside too.

Art in the kitchen

View of a guest room

This feels more like a **home than a hotel**, and it is family-owned and run.

At first sight, it is as if a sea gypsy lives here, a seafaring collector and hoarder of curios from around the world, having sailed perhaps from Scandinavia to Tahiti and back again. Everywhere there are brightly painted model boats, statues and sculptures, pieces of coral, ceramics, beachcomber pieces punctuated with books, an informal and accessible library on art, travel, design, photography. The comfortable, artful interior is filled with inviting furniture, paintings and plants, lit up by day with the sun, at night by an enviable collection of architectural lamps.

This feels more like a home than a hotel, and it is family-owned and run. However, it has been purposefully designed, rather than just a private house recently opened up to paying guests. Architect Marco de Luca and his wife Eugenia di Leva have made over what was once a restaurant into a small very stylish Mediterranean hotel, with only a dozen rooms that are more like suites. Each has floor-to-ceiling windows for gazing at the bay and village below; each is different from the others; all are colorful, immaculately detailed and cleverly accessorized. You will investigate your surroundings with much interest and pleasure. Even the handles on doors and cupboards are distinctive. And it seems that every alcove, shelf and bookcase in the passageways and stairwells has an intriguing tableau to study.

The large living room, sun-worshipper terraces and kitchen are all exclusive to the guests, who can easily separate themselves from others around about the spacious shared areas of La Minervetta. Halfway down the cliff, stairs lead to a rectangular wedge of land that juts out, green with grass: in its center a cooling Jacuzzi, ideal for summer refreshing.

Breakfast – decoratively served and deliciously tasty – is served inside or out on the terrace; in the evening, pre-dinner drinks placed on a tray. It is just 15 minutes from here to walk to Sorrento's many restaurants and bars, along the winding road above or five minutes down the winding private path to those at the seaside neighborhood laid out below. Choosing this latter option, but unable to decide what to have from the menu, we thankfully agreed that the persuasive Luisa of family-owned and staffed restaurant La Delfina should choose dinner for us – much simpler, with a great result. The walk back up is a certain fitness test.

Detail of living room

The living room

La Minervetta, centered on the cliff

La Minervetta is central on the Amalfi Coast, described as the world's most beautiful coastline. It is an impossibly lovely vista of ancient towns that cling to sheer black volcanic rock cliffs, with blue seas far below and most often blue skies above. Oak, chestnut, pine, olive and lemon trees thrive in its historic soil. Sorrento is the source of Limoncello, the local lemon liqueur that has gone global. Its fresh cool taste is like the essence of early summer in a glass. This too is where the stylish sleek motorboats often seen in movies have been made since the 1950s, and the sturdy unsinkable fishing boats.

From here, it is easy to visit the city of Naples for the day, or the tragic Roman town of Pompeii, forever preserved after the eruption of Vesuvius in 79 BC buried it in ash. In half an hour you can be ferried to the small and lovely island of Capri – the preferred holiday spot of emperors Tiberius and Augustus, conquerors in their turn conquered by nature.

The beach

Not only emperors, but also poets, painters, writers and musicians have been inspired by the landscape. The Sorrentine Peninsula was part of the "Grand Tour," for foreign intellectuals and dilettantes studying the art, history and culture of Italy – many never went home. A fusion of Byzantine, Moorish and Roman architecture can be seen in a collection of convents, churches, cloisters, villas and palaces. Piazzas, gardens, galleries and museums are threaded through the terrain. By car, it is a spectacular and at times breathtakingly narrow drive around the coast.

From your La Minervetta eyrie, you have a bird's-eye view of the coastline; in fact you are so high up that seagulls fly below the windows. From your room or the terrace, you are looking out across an ancient amphitheater, a scene that has been admired for centuries. In Greek legend, sirens lived on the Sorrento coast: beautiful mermaid-like creatures singing songs that enchanted and lured sailors in to the shore, then forever under their spell. There is a sculpture of a siren at La Minervetta. It calls us back, as it will you.

View of Marina Grande and Sorrento

View from the terrace across the Bay of Naples

La Minervetta Maison
Sorrento
Italy

Tel: (39 051) 877-4455
Fax: (39 051) 878-4601
E-mail: info@laminervetta.com
Internet: www.laminervetta.com

The keyport of the Hotel Danieli

Grand Finale

Hotel Danieli   Venice, Italy

These gold keys with their scarlet silk tassels open the door to the Byzantine charm of a 14th-century Venetian palace; and by virtue of possession, entry to this mysterious "studied, sly, enslaving" city.

Arriving in Venice for a second visit, I am struck by the same feeling of slight unease. It is an almost physical alertness to something not quite right, some out-of-kilter nervous response. My self-diagnosis is that I am experiencing the "Looking Glass" effect, crossing, like Alice through a mirror, into the myriad paintings and sketches depicting Venice that I have absorbed over the years. That sense of dislocation, the contemporary inserted into an historical envelope, is disconcerting until the familiar signs of modern life direct a return to reality.

The front door of the Hotel Danieli

Yet some there be
by due steps aspire
To lay their just hands on
**that golden key that
opens the palace**
of Eternity.
John Milton

My first visit was 10 years ago, in winter, when the shopkeepers open for business greeted me with mild surprise. Like migratory birds, tourists were expected with the warmer weather. Now, more and more people winter in Venice to avoid the summer crowds. But this is a city invaded daily, weekly and monthly by the hordes seeking to discover the legend for themselves. As a result, there are few moments when you have Venice to yourself: perhaps on an early morning when, glimpsed from a gondola or water-taxi, the city floats mirage-like on quiet waters; or at sunset as day-trippers retreat from the cluster of islands and the palace of the doges is flushed a deeper pink. Inhabitants appear ambivalent about the invasion of their city, but while tourism is their livelihood, Venice is in danger of being trampled into the lagoon's quiet waters.

The Hotel Danieli's terracotta-and-white arched façade has been a Venetian landmark for 600 years. Entering the enveloping front doors is another step back in time. The interiors probably looked very much the same when guests stayed centuries ago, although modern amenities have been added.

The palace was once the home of Venetian nobles, the Dandolo family. One of its most famous sons, Enrico Dandolo, conquered Constantinople in 1205, and brought back gold, marble and other treasures with him, including four horses. These now-famous bronze animals stand above the entry of the Basilica di San Marco in Venice's busiest square.

The distinctive terracotta façade of the Hotel Danieli and winter gondolas

The golden staircase

The Hall Dandolo

The Danieli's lobby opens onto a magnificent atrium, with a grand staircase of gold marble leading up to the suites and guest rooms, all furnished in Empire style with precious antique pieces. The most opulent of these is the princely Doge's Suite.

Hung with chandeliers crafted on Murano, the island center of the Venetian glass-making industry, the Hall Dandolo is a splendid setting for the simple ritual of afternoon tea, which may seem too prosaic an activity in this soaring poetic space.

Suite 36

A city of more than 118 islands, linked by a labyrinthine fretwork of footbridges and canals, Venice was once a mighty maritime nation. Every Ascension Day, to symbolize the marriage between city and sea, the doge would sail his golden barge from the lagoon to cast a wedding ring into the Adriatic, symbolizing the marriage of Venice to the sea. This 700-year-old ritual is re-enacted on the Grand Canal each September with a regatta of richly decorated patrician gondolas.

Although its grandeur has faded, Venice continues to reign, if only over the imaginations of those drawn to her colorful and prosperous past.

Last frame – the view of the lagoon and the Church of Santa Maria della Salute from the terrace

Hotel Danieli
Venice
Italy
Tel: (39 41) 52226480
Fax: (39 41) 5200208
Internet: www.danieli.hotelinvenice.com

The Mosaic, entrance to the gardens of Villa d'Este

Dolce Vita

Lake Como, Italy

One of the quintessential grand hotels of Europe, set in magnificent Renaissance gardens on the edge of Lake Como, Villa d'Este has a romantic history worthy of an opera.

The gardens, planted when the estate was created in 1568, are wonderfully established. In the 10 acre private park of Villa d'Este, carpets of lawns are punctuated with Italian cypresses, magnolias, horse chestnuts and well-placed statues. The magnificent centerpiece is the 18th-century mosaic, classed as an Italian national treasure. Its appealing symmetry screens an outdoor room with a central fish pond. Beyond, two rows of cypress trees lead up the hill past a cascade of fountains to the Grotto of Hercules. Behind it, thick woodlands overlook the deep waters of Lake Como.

From here it is a short climb to the fortifications, a collection of battlements and towers built by a woman to amuse a man. Soon after the death of her elderly husband, the Marquis Calderara, the ballerina La Pelusina, then the owner of Villa d'Este, remarried a young Napeolonic general. Worried that he might feel nostalgic for warring, she gave him his own fort to keep him at home, and he happily played soldiers here. Now it gives guests somewhere to walk to and exercise off the splendid food.

The lobby

The classic façade of the Queen's Building at Villa d'Este, built in 1856, named after Princess Caroline, wife of George IV. Terracotta, with trompe l'oeil shutters and trim, the annex's deep red façade is decorated with emblems of the Italian provinces.

Villa d'Este from Lake Como

Villa d'Este is a legendary hotel, and has been described as "not a hotel where you just stay, it's a hotel where you settle." It draws its guests from the upper reaches of the old and new European and American societies. Lake Como lured Greeks and Romans, Celts and Renaissance Europeans years before Americans and the Hollywood "aristocracy" discovered it. Cardinals and princesses have also lived here and it has been a welcome refuge for royalty and for revolutionaries. The Princess of Wales – Princess Caroline of Brunswick, the unhappy wife of King George IV – lived here for five years from 1815 to 1820, and the Empress Maria Fedorowna, wife of the Russian tsar, rented the villa for two weeks in 1868 and then ended up staying for two years.

The main building of Villa d'Este is a white neoclassical palazzo, from the 16th-century, designed by the architect Pellegrino Pellegrini. Enter through a narrow revolving door and you arrive in the 16th-century lobby, a blue and gold salon with marble floors, vaulted ceilings and Murano glass chandeliers. There is a gentle grandeur throughout; the furniture is usually Empire, upholstered in silk and velvet, and antique accessories are everywhere. However, this is not a museum, in either its furnishings or mood.

Here still is the grand European-style service, but without the old pomp and circumstance: you are made welcome, and the hotel feels gracious and serene, with an opulence that is natural, not fake, and comfortable, not formal. Take the double marble staircase or the elevator lined in Como silk brocade to your gracious and generously proportioned room. The shutters are opened on your arrival, so you may admire the stunning view from the balcony, one said to have inspired the invention of photography. This is a lake of legendary allure, its majestic beauty an attraction to visitors since Roman times. Ringed by mountains, its placid waters are constantly ruffled by sailing boats, water-taxis, ferries and water-skiers. Lake Como is circled with the grand villas of the aristocracy and the newly rich and famous. Little villages in ice-cream colors sit at its green edges, and all are best seen from the water.

Here you can be pampered and calmed, only 30 minutes from the bustle of Milan, in this place for lovers – of gardens, and of elegance, and of each other.

Suite Room

You can take the Villa's private launch or hire one of the sleek wooden motorboats to visit the beautiful villages of Bellagio and Varenna, or you can be perfectly content to sit on the terrace and enjoy the view. While it is romantic, it is not merely chocolate box pretty. The tranquillity is tempered with the drama of mountains, and the light changes constantly.

The Veranda restaurant salon opens on each side to the sculpted gardens and, at the front, to the lake – where best to sit is the first decision. Next is the choice of divine food with painterly presentation and heavenly flavors. Here you may eat the food and then buy Villa d'Este's deluxe recipe book, or attend cookery classes presided over by the master chef. Visiting to take lunch, or dinner, would be a reasonable compromise if you were not able to stay here. After lunch, wander the manicured gardens and paths, walk under the arcades covered with jasmine and wisteria, watch the lake from the terrace with its plane trees; one, in the middle of the terrace, is more than 600 years old. For the more energetic, there is a health club discreetly placed in the grounds. A heated swimming pool floats lazily on the lake, its teak decks moving with the swell like a boat.

The Canova Room

Villa d'Este has a long pedigree and a celebrated guest list. The words "grand hotel" evoke another era, more gracious and less hurried than our own. Keeping up with the times can be difficult, however, and not every grand hotel is as grand as it once was. Much stays the same at Villa d'Este but it has moved itself from being an old to a new grand hotel, proving that things that were great can continue to be so. Consistently voted one of the world's top hotels, it gives considerable value for the considerable money it costs to stay here. This is a place to spoil yourself, an ultimate and memorable extravagance, and a delicious slice of la dolce vita.

The teak-decked swimming pool floats on the lake

Villa d'Este
Lago Como
Italy
Tel: (39 31) 3481
Fax: (39 31) 348844
E-mail: info@villadeste.it
Internet: www.villadeste.it

Urban Retreat

| The Tawaraya Inn | Kyoto, Japan |

The Tawaraya turns away from the street to face inward to privacy, peace and serenity. In a modern city with its share of urban chaos, tranquillity rules in this ryokan. Nearly 300 years old, the traditional Japanese inn is dignified but not paralyzed by the past.

The attributes of modern living are here but gracefully hidden, carefully shrouded in beautiful textiles or placed in containers that hide their form. You, honored guest, also have your special place in this ordered environment. Other than a small and beautiful library that I'd like transplanted to my own home, there are no public spaces where you might confront other guests. Often, you encounter no one – even the staff seem to materialize rather than exist. Only room-service food is available, but what food to stay in for. And there is the exquisite fussing of the staff, serenely mannered but ever alert to your smallest needs.

The exterior of the Tawaraya

The reception

In a plain, narrow street in central Kyoto you can take refuge behind the Tawaraya's walls, embrace solitude or enjoy companionship, contemplate, rest, be restored.

A pervading air of calm provides a sanctuary from the relentless race of contemporary life. Here are the real luxuries of silence, space and gourmet food – asceticism without sacrifice. Traditional Japanese architecture and innkeeping combine, providing a marvellous experience that is relevant and viable. Refined, luxurious, it is essentially a simple way of life, ordered and arranged.

Within these walls, the guest is the focus. You must submit to the routine and rhythms that are the ritual of staying in a ryokan. This is not an experience for those of harried temperament. Be prepared to adjust to the formality, the service and manners that are unlike any other style of hotel. Your role is that of honored guest.

Having left your shoes and donned slippers at the entrance, you shed your travel clothes, and choose from the wardrobe of special kimonos and yukatas in your room. Slide back the shoji screens to contemplate the serene private gardens – with a stone pool where water flows from a bamboo tap into the stone basin below, leafy maple trees and moss-covered stone lanterns.

Rooms are simple, gracefully decorated with traditional furniture, and some Western pieces for those who find it hard to sit on the floor. Traditional tatami matting is laid on the floor, sumptuous brocades cover the telephone and other reminders of the real world.

Your room is dual purpose, by day a living and dining room, at night transformed into a bedroom when a futon is made up for you.

The bathroom is an essay in contrast – you can soak and relax in a traditional Japanese bath, a deep cedar tub kept constantly full of hot water by apparently invisible attendants, or marvel at the high-tech toilet with its array of flashing lights and symbols, appropriately hidden from view.

The evening banquet looked too beautiful to eat. Visually stunning compositions are served by our smiling kimono-clad lady-in-waiting who appears on soundless slippered feet, as if from out of the walls rather than through sliding doors.

Room service

The Gyosuan (morning light) Room

The bathroom

Presented on delicate Japanese pottery, each dish tastes exquisite. I start writing down a description of the courses in order to remember them but several sakes later both my handwriting and descriptive abilities become blurred. I can no longer focus even with what must be the world's most beautiful hotel stationery and pens at my disposal.

Our 10-course dinner is cooked, arranged and served with absolute artistry. It culminates with a simple grapefruit jelly served in a grapefruit shell framed by its porcelain dish – a dessert that deserves to be enshrined.

This is followed by a deepest sleep in the softest futon after which you are woken with morning newspapers and pots of tea.

Beautiful objects and changing table scenes in the corridors of the hotel reflect the seasons and events: May 5, horse racing; April, cherry blossom time; November, autumn leaves...

Authenticity, or at least the illusion of authenticity, combines with luxury and service to harness past and present into a harmonious parallel.

Here you are surrounded by people who ease out the little inconveniences that make or mar the quality of life. They minister to the needs of guests with ceremony and elegance: service is an art form. Your lasting memories will be of the faultless manners that characterize this other-world Kyoto. That alone is worth the considerable expense. To be treated with such distinction, no matter who you are, invites mirror behavior. A taste of old-world courtesy and the opportunity to practice it yourself is another gain.

The Satow family has owned the Tawaraya Inn for 11 generations and it is now run, with gentle precision, by Mrs. Toshi Okazaki Satow.

The Fuji Room from the garden – looking in at peace

If you must venture out ...

Kyoto is the ancient imperial capital, and it is here that the classic image of Japan survives. Behind the walls of the renowned temples, shrines, imperial villas and gardens is the traditional calm of Japanese culture. It hides behind the frenetic urban sprawl, with its traffic, neon signs, shopping arcades, crowded streets and pachinko parlours. The geisha quarter of Gion was the setting for Arthur Golden's book *Memoirs of a Geisha*.

In the busy streets, swirling masses of young Japanese girls chatter and laugh into their tiny pastel cell phones.

The Ten-you restaurant, a branch of the Tawaraya, is only two minutes' walk for a tempura lunch or dinner, or there is the famous Kawamichiya noodle shop.

You will return to your refuge with a sense of relief, ready for its seductive shot of calmness and tranquillity in an otherwise frantic life. The ryokan's enclosed world is perfect for restoring balance after an excursion into this hectic city. A willing capitulation to the order of the ryokan encourages you to slow down and surrender the tension you arrived with.

Departure is a ceremony in itself. The staff farewell sees the taxi out of sight, vesting the departure with such dignity you determine to return, to be treated again as the honored guest.

The Tawaraya Inn
Kyoto
Japan
Tel: (81 75) 211-5566
Fax: (81 75) 211-2204

In the Neighborhood

The Condesa DF Hotel   Mexico City, Mexico

Sunday afternoon in the floating gardens of Xochimilico: battalions of brightly painted boats crowd the canals, jostling for position and, much like the traffic of Mexico City, prone to gridlock as "lanes converge."

Drifting in convoy, propelled by pole, an excursion on these Mexican gondolas is like being at a fairground that floats. The boats themselves are silent; the noise and color come from the gaudy paint schemes and the festive family atmosphere on the water. Music boats carry mariachi and marimba bands, and folk-singing *norteños*, mixed among the Mexican families and visitors on a day out. As they move along the waterways, they can beckon to the bandleaders if they want to hire some music to dine by, and the music float comes alongside. Of course people in nearby boats can hear the music for free, songs you might enjoy or have to suffer while being in the vicinity. Your boatman could pole your craft faster, and soon other music will drift by you.

Picnic baskets brought from home can provide lunch fare, but takeout on the water is also available. Darting in among the gaps of the colorful convoys, looking for customers, are little cafés; narrow low-in-the-water boats fitted with small gas stoves, ready to sell you an enchilada "to go," made as you watch, and grilled or boiled corn cobs. Shops selling flowers and souvenirs float by too.

A chatter of voices, laughter and music; primary, even neon colors: the cheerful sounds and sights of a leisurely afternoon boating just an hour from the center of the world's biggest city.

Boats at Xochimilico

Looking down from the rooftop terrace

Altitude and attitude: while the air is definitely thinner here, at some 7,400 feet (2,255 m) above sea level, the outlook for this ancient and once great Aztec city is more positive now, the issue of its sinking *Centro Historico* apart. Sprawling, crowded, beset by smog, crime and traffic – like many other conurbations – contemporary Mexico City is also a cosmopolitan party town with a thriving art scene attracting international interest and money. And, like so many cities, it is less of one entity and more a collection of neighborhoods.

Popular with the "art crowd," and named after the quiet neighborhood it is in, the Condesa DF Hotel has a festive air once you are inside the circa 1928 Parisian-style building. There is a feeling that a party might spontaneously combust. Perhaps it is the perky color scheme and contemporary design, or the interesting mix of guests and locals in its busy restaurants and bars: whatever, the atmosphere is immediately appealing. The place is constantly and pleasantly active, all day. After work, the bars upstairs and downstairs start to fill with people, and late in the evening the dance club in the basement fires up. The overall mood is relaxed, easygoing, yet dynamic; and it is a great place to people-watch.

The spectacular – and dizzying – view from the top to the ground floor reveals the clever insertion of a new interior into an old exterior. Each floor has a walk-along balcony that overlooks the inner patio, a shaded and cool space modeled after those of Mexican haciendas. Shutters along the balconies filter the light, creating an interesting chiaroscuro effect. Local and Mexican architect Javier Sanchez was responsible for the restoration and Parisian India Mahdavi for the interior spaces and chic overall design. There is a generous use of turquoise in many of the spaces, tempered with white and yellow, resulting in a fresh, crisp scheme that is both calming and energizing.

The Condesa exterior

The patio bar

From the rooftop terrace and bar, the view is a leafy one, looking down to tree-lined streets and across to the lush Parque Espa a – and at night, into the living rooms of some interesting apartments as their occupants return home and turn on their lights. From this vantage point, the air is fresh and clear, and the swirling traffic below irrelevant. On a balmy summer night this is the place to be. If there is a chill in the air, white woven rugs are there to wrap up in. The food served up here is, somewhat surprisingly, sushi; delicious tastes expertly made and overseen by a Japanese sushi chef lured from New York. A tiny spa and splash pool is cleverly hidden on this level, and a gym, so you can work out as well as eat out.

The rooftop bar

The view from the rooms, unless you have a suite with its own private balcony, is onto the streets below, but the room itself is very pleasing, with a comfortable sitting room as well as bedroom. Sliding doors can close off the entrance hall to the bedroom, as well as the sitting room, the bathroom and the windows. Soft colors with walnut wood paneling, linen and leather-covered furniture, and a large desk make it a cool sanctuary when you need to rest up from being out and about in this chaotic but exciting city.

The Condesa has the best "in-room" book encountered so far; full of useful information ordered in cleverly designed but easy to access "pockets," and a simple, very effective idea – a map of the *barrio*, the neighborhood, highlighting the things to see. Interesting buildings, cafés, restaurants, shops and art galleries in the immediate vicinity are marked and numbered. Condesa the neighborhood has been a trendy arts district of the city, and although many of the resident artists and galleries have moved on, as the area has become more popular and expensive, it still has an attractively bohemian air.

From this vantage point, the air is **fresh and clear**, and the swirling traffic below irrelevant.

Inside Room X-III

Late nights are the norm in this city, so breakfasts can easily run on into lunch; the comfort of the breakfast rooms encourages lounging about rather than hurrying out. Not many people seem to be in a rush. Condi, the hotel's Labrador, wearing his color-coordinated neckkerchief, is often found asleep in the lobby or under the banquette seats in the breakfast area, although is always willing to be lively company on a walk. There are plenty of places to while away time inside the hotel. Browsing in the library through the many books on Mexican history, culture and art give insight to the country's rich and often chaotic past; the boutique shop has many temptations to consider taking home.

Inside the Condesa is colorful, but armed with the map you should wander out and around the neighborhood. It too is colorful; streets are punctuated by brightly painted buildings that stand out against the usual gray, with architecture that is a spot-the-era mixture of Spanish Colonial,

Condi, the hotel Labrador

Breakfast and lounge bar

Street stall, local cuisine

The Angel of Independence

Art Deco and slick contemporary. The greenery of trees and parks accent the scheme, and there is a great mix of design stores – look out for Artefacto and the memorably named Chic by Accident – cafés, street food stalls and nightlife.

Not everyone who comes to Mexico visits its capital. Many just pass through the airport in transit to the country's beach resorts and colonial towns.

But to write off Mexico City for its size (20 million inhabitants and growing), or its reputation (not as tarnished as it was) would be to miss out on experiencing one of the oldest and most diverse capital cities in the world. Its many neighborhoods are almost like separate towns within this huge city, each with its own different personality and attractions. Wherever you go during the day or evening in Mexico City, you will happily return to the haven of the Condesa, and the welcome of Condi and his team.

The Condesa DF Hotel
Mexico City
Mexico
Tel: (52 55) 5241-2600
E-mail: info@condesadf.com
Internet: www.condesadf.com

The Ambassade Hotel stretches along the Herengracht

On the Waterfront

| The Ambassade Hotel | Amsterdam, The Netherlands |

In what is one of the world's great cities on water, the Ambassade Hotel is canal-side, a priority in choosing a place to stay in Amsterdam. Situated in the historical center of Amsterdam on the Herengracht (Gentleman's Canal) the hotel has a peaceful setting slightly off the major tourist track. Yet it is close to good cafés, restaurants and bookshops, to the many museums, the floating flower market and shopping streets. Nearby is the tree-lined Jordaan area, an old neighborhood undergoing a renovation renaissance, and on almost every street there seems to be an Indonesian restaurant, reflecting the legacy of Dutch explorers and spice traders who journeyed back and forth to what was once called New Holland.

The Ambassade is a row of gabled centuries-old canal houses. On a charmingly small scale, the 10 buildings are cobbled together as a hotel. Each is four or five storeys high, with steep staircases, twisting corridors, and low-beamed ceilings. No designer drew this hotel up: it has evolved in its own eccentric way. The Ambassade has a literary tradition, reflected in names signed in the visitor's book. The hotel is apparently favored by writers such as Oliver Sacks, Salman Rushdie and John Le Carré. No doubt many were on book-promoting gigs in the city. There is soon to be a hotel library, to house the many books signed by the author guests.

The Sitting Room

The hotel is discreetly signed, and blends well into the essentially residential area. Despite being made up of 10 houses, it is comparatively small, with none of its 52 rooms alike. This is an elegant individual and friendly hotel. The ornate breakfast room overlooking the canal serves a generous traditional Dutch repast. Because it is such a pleasant and spacious room, with white lacquered walls and two-storey-high windows, it is better to forgo room service and eat here. The antique-filled sitting room next door is a good location to enjoy a leisurely mid-morning coffee or an afternoon drink, admiring the old and ornate walnut clock with its moving fleet of ships.

Our room looked out over the canal. The large windows opened wide on the early autumn afternoon, letting in the still warm sun. Just above the street and heads of passersby, the room had a gracious and welcoming feel, the atmosphere of a comfortable home. The bed was placed in an alcove, with table and chairs placed beside the window, adding to the impression of being in a living room. With a glass of wine and food bought from a nearby café, we sat and watched Amsterdam go by. The boat traffic along the canal is a reminder that this is a maritime city and major port. There was also a constant stream of cars and bicycles, and the sound of murmuring Amsterdammers headed for cafés, to visit friends, or going home …

At night, the city's bridges, illuminated by tiny lights placed around their arches, seem suspended over a void until a boat comes by with its lights on. The huge variety of boats range from the trim to the wallowing-noisy tourist craft, a wooden dinghy being rowed to a nearby restaurant, barges motoring by on business, homes afloat and vessels tied up by their owners who are refueling at a convenient café ... The Ambassade's added water attraction is a massage center with flotation tanks. It provides a pleasant remedy for stress and jetlag, and perhaps writer's block.

Think of an archery target and you have a bead on Amsterdam, laid out within concentric circles formed by its five main canals. The web of smaller waterways within brings the total number to 160 canals, the city claiming to have more canals than Venice. Traversing these watery barriers are 1,281 bridges, negotiated by 550,000 bicycles and even more cars.

Original beams in Attic bedroom number 68

The gable of the first house of the Ambassade's ten

The Café 'T Smalle, a short stroll or sail from the hotel

Renting a bike is an option if you prefer your own wheels, but Amsterdam is a city to enjoy on foot. At night, uncurtained interiors offer glimpses of how the citizens live, contemporary versions of Vermeer's light-infused canvasses, which captured everyday Dutch scenes in the 17th century.

Cruising the grand canals in a rented motorboat is a rather more elegant alternative to a two-seater water bike. Tourist boats provide a seafarer's perspective on houses built along the canal banks by wealthy mariners during the prosperous age of merchant sail. Famed for museums focused on art – Van Gogh, the Rijksmuseum with its Rembrandts and Vermeers and the modern art of the Stedelijk – Amsterdam also caters to more down-to-earth tastes with museums specializing in subjects as diverse as trams, beer, sex and football. Something for everyone ...

The modern and the medieval coexist comfortably in this very cosmopolitan city. Fans of architecture should see the quirky apartment complex of Eigen Haard (Our Hearth), on Michel de Klerk's drawing board from 1913 to 1920. The striking Science Centre New Metropolis by Renzo Piano rises like an ocean liner from the harbor and there is cutting-edge design from the appropriately named radical Dutch architect Rem Koolhaas. Check out Architectura & Natura, a specialized bookstore at Leliegracht 44, for guidebooks on modern Dutch buildings.

Amsterdam has a 400-year association with diamonds. It is also linked with tulips, which have their own fascinating history. As the Ambassade Hotel has a connection with writers, it seems fitting to mention two excellent books featuring tulips, one a novel, the other a history.

The Amsterdam of the early 17th century was immortalized in seemingly serene domestic interiors painted by Vermeer and Rembrandt. Deborah Moggach's book *Tulip Fever* adds another dimension to the artists' canvases. Set in 1630s Amsterdam, a typical renaissance love triangle draws a wealthy elderly merchant, his beautiful but frustrated young wife, and the painter commissioned to paint the couple's portrait. The artist becomes entangled in a series of emotional and financial speculations, including tulip-bulb trading, and the lives of the three central characters are utterly changed. The text is interspersed with 16 beautifully reproduced Dutch paintings, a novel addition to this work of fiction.

A gardening writer, Anna Pavord has recorded the bizarre history of the tulip in *The Tulip*, a massive book that is both scholarly and entertaining. Originating in Central Asia, tulips were transported to Europe by the Turks. In the 1730s the Dutch were overtaken by "tulipomania," with single bulbs changing hands for the price of a house. Other countries including France caught the tulip fever. While the Europeans eventually regained their composure, the tulip's popularity now reaches out to embrace the New World. Pavord's book is illustrated with hundreds of full page prints of the stylish flower.

The Ambassade Hotel

Amsterdam
The Netherlands

Tel: (31 20) 626-2333
Fax: (31 20) 624-5321
E-mail: info@ambassade-hotel.nl
Internet: www.ambassade-hotel.nl

Pride of Place

Eichardt's   Queenstown, New Zealand

"It is a truth universally acknowledged, that a single man in possession of a good fortune must be in want of a wife." Or so Jane Austen wrote in the opening sentence of her novel *Pride and Prejudice*.

In real-life a former Prussian Guard put that "truth" into gender reverse. Around 1865, Mr. Albert Eichardt arrived in New Zealand to try his luck on the gold fields. As fate would have it, he met a single woman in possession of a good fortune. Miss Julia Shanahan owned a hotel on the edge of a picturesque lake in Queenstown. Albert and Julia married, and Eichardt's became the name of their now jointly owned hotel.

Their marriage and the hotel prospered. By 1873, a landmark building of stone and brick, Italian in design, was in place. It was described as "very ornate, and really superb in appearance." Eichardt's was the first building to have electricity in Queenstown, some 30 years before the rest of the town. In 1890, Mr. and Mrs. Eichardt could boast a hotel with "70 rooms all lighted by electricity."

They would have not foreseen the glittering and electric town that Queenstown is now, nor that their hotel would become the gem that it is. Eichardt's Private Hotel no longer has so many rooms, but it is still the lakefront landmark.

Twilight over Queenstown and Lake Wakatipu

Eichardt's Hotel from the lake

Queenstown is now often described as being the "adrenalin capital" of the world. It certainly started with a rush. In 1862, gold was found and within six months the population escalated from just 12 to 8,500 people. There was soon a sea of tents by the waterfront – Canvastown was its early name. The town's setting, flanking a beautiful lake edged by majestic mountains, was considered spectacular. It was said to be a view and place "fit for a Queen." The tribute became its lasting name.

Eichardt's began in a simple building. When the bustling tent town sprang up, a woolshed was turned into a hotel to cater to thirsty gold miners. It soon became too small, and a tent was put up beside it as extra space. However, the tent leaked when it rained, customers complained, and so a more solid building program began. Additions and renovations were made as the town and Eichardt's business thrived. The hotel became the center of the town's social life. But, over time, the hotel's fortunes waned. It survived neglect, competition, floods and demolition plans. When the present owners bought it, it was a rundown tavern. A huge restoration program was put in place to restore it to its once "superb appearance."

The iconic structure is now spruced up inside and out. A glass and steel atrium extension gives a contemporary entrance with a historical reference: its style alluding to both the classic shape of a woolshed and the openness of a tent. The original building's façade was restored, the interior transformed. Now there are just five suites. Eichardt's is a small luxury hotel with a history, and a sense of space inside that belies its exterior. Its prime corner and lakefront frontage means that guests step outside straight into the lively night and day scene of Queenstown. The best restaurants, cafés and shops – and a cinema – are all but a minute or three's walk from the front door.

The Parlor

Interior detail

The hotel lobby

There is a **great interplay of textures**; metal and velvet, fur and wood are all combined.

The striking black, brown and white theme of the light-filled lobby is a crisp, smart foil to the steel framing and glass. Its layering of textures, symmetry and detailing is a first sign that this is an interior that has been deftly designed.

The suites and a guest parlor are upstairs in the original building. In the suites, a soft dark-chocolate background with shots of cream and orange makes a soothing and rich environment. The rooms are classical, but have

Bedroom of suite

a definite opulence. A fire adds glow, and from the balcony the view across over and far down Lake Wakatipu to the mountain peaks of the Remarkables is simply stunning.

There is a great interplay of textures; metal and velvet, fur and wood are all combined. The suite is detailed and layered but not to excess. Comfort is paramount. The eagle insignia you might notice on the sofa cushion is a subtle link back to Albert Eichardt; it is the emblem of the Prussian guards.

The private parlor is vibrant, luxurious and Victorian in feel, with clever references to the town's and the region's historic gold mining heritage. Breakfast is served here, or in your room if you prefer. French toast with lemon and maple syrup, scrambled eggs: whatever you would like is cooked for you.

Suite sitting room

Arriving at Eichardt's

Downstairs, the House bar – and café – is one of the best places to be, out of your room. It is a stylish yet casual meeting spot, a favorite with locals, and popular for lunch, serving tasty dishes like risotto – confit of duck with mushrooms, snowpeas and parmesan – and wild venison pie with a blueberry relish. For dinner, there are plenty of restaurants to choose from, just as there is plenty to do when you are here.

Hurl yourself off a bridge or cliff if you must, or go hang-gliding, jet boating, white-water rafting. Take the "trilogy trail" to tour some of the *Lord of the Rings* movie locations. You can go on day trips, or stroll up the street to Joe's Garage for a shot of coffee. Craft galleries, design and clothing stores are just on and around the corner. For skiers, the fields at Coronet Peak, the Remarkables and Cardrona are all within an hour's drive from the hotel. Apres-ski, or instead of, pay a visit to the vineyards. This is the most southern winemaking area in the world, and renowned for its pinot noir. An excursion on the vintage steamship TSS *Earnslaw* gives a great view of this very scenic location.

"Staying in" is a tempting option, cosseted in your very attractive room, away from the external action options. Inside, you can explore peace and quiet; the farthest you need leap is up and down the stairs. Still in pride of place, Eichardt's is a jewel, the gold that Albert Eichardt truly found, and worthy again of its special setting.

The TSS *Earnslaw* on Lake Wakatipu

Skier at Coronet Peak

Eichardt's

Queenstown
New Zealand

Tel: (64 3) 441-0450
Fax: (64 3) 441-0440
E-mail: enquiries@eichardtshotel.co.nz
Internet: www.eichardtshotel.co.nz

Royal Welcome

Greenhill – The Lodge   Hawke's Bay, New Zealand

Imagine you were the owner of this lovely old house and you were told to expect a very special visitor; not one you had actually invited, but one to whom you were unable to refuse your hospitality, as a loyal subject. Monarchy, in the form of the Queen of England's mother, will be arriving to stay. Her Majesty had expressed a wish to experience life in a genuine farmhouse, albeit just for 48 hours. Yours was deemed the best in the area, so the Government chose it, giving you just a few weeks to get everything in right royal order.

This polite command was given just before Christmas of 1957. Despite the timing, it was decided that both inside and out must be given a thorough makeover. A suite of rooms was cleared of the family's possessions and completely redecorated, the rest of the furnishings renovated and spring-cleaned although it was the height of a Southern Hemisphere summer. Carpets were beaten, paintwork washed, lawns and gardens manicured; all made spick and span. Queen Elizabeth the Queen Mother arrived to stay at Greenhill in February of 1958.

That was many years ago, but spic and span it still is, although no longer a farmhouse. Greenhill is now a small and exclusive hotel, one with the feeling of a luxurious private home. It is an elegant comfortable house in the heart of wine country, with a touch of regal graciousness that would have suited its royal guest.

The dining room

Greenhill was **grand** in its first days of 1900, and has only improved with age.

Greenhill was grand in its first days of 1900 and has only improved with age. Built of heart totara from a nearby forest, and with its original matai timber flooring and paneling intact, this classic old house is a fine example of high Victorian architecture. Its ornate pressed zinc ceilings were imported from Britain; no expense was spared in its decoration, befitting its first and newly wealthy owner. Now it has a collection of contemporary New Zealand art and ceramics, and an assortment of furniture that has evolved to an eclectic yet coherent interior style. The balconied turret is more a fancy or a folly than serving any real purpose, but it gives a splendid view over the surrounding countryside. It must have been gratifying for the original homestead owner to survey his land from up here, a terrain stretching as far as the eye could see.

Now there is far more garden than farmland surrounding the lodge, and in the distance, acres of vineyards, source of the crisp whites and soft reds, wines that Hawke's Bay is rightly famous for, both in New Zealand and beyond. This is fertile country; fruits and vegetables flourish in its temperate climate, as do grapes, and creative juices flow here too. Traveling the local arts and crafts trail and visiting the farmers' markets will bring you back to Greenhill loaded with bounty.

The region's culinary wealth is very well displayed in the cuisine served at the lodge. You can taste the best of the wine and food available, in an exclusive dining room and, afterward, retire to the living room, or the billiard room and then to bed.

Sitting room detail

Living room of the Villa Suite

The Billiard Room

An historic rambling garden, being restored to much of its former glory, gives Greenhill a park-like setting. An avenue of oaks and elms leads up to the house on the hill, and among the many notable trees are a magnificent almond, German medlar and Japanese pagoda tree.

Although its traditional style has been kept and enhanced, Greenhill is equipped with the contemporary comforts and technology that 21st-century guests expect. A fitness center has transformed what were once the stables, a swimming pool and croquet court has replaced what were servants' quarters.

Suites and rooms are as elegant as you would expect, each with a small sitting room and doors opening out onto the balcony. The historic Queen Mother's suite is now a favorite. The quiet of the country and privacy of the location delivers a deep sleep. There is a separate villa as part of the property, more 60s contemporary in style, with the same comforts and

Art Deco weekend in Napier

Napier Art Deco architecture

only a minute's walk from the main house. Sequestered away here, there is total privacy and a bucolic view over farmland. You can make your own dinner if you wish, or have a chef cook it for you.

As well as wine richness, there is architectural wealth here too. Nearby is the city of Napier. After a massive earthquake in 1931, it was reduced to ruins and razed to the ground. With the past destroyed, planners and architects rebuilt in a new modernist style, Art Deco. Years later, there is nowhere else where such a range of buildings in the style is preserved in such a concentrated area. The third week of every February is a magnet for Deco enthusiasts worldwide, a long weekend celebrating the era in high style.

Crowds of people dressed in 30s' finery stroll the streets, party at concerts, balls and supper dances, drive by in vintage cars and dine out at the many cafés and restaurants. Guides wearing striped blazers and boaters lead tours of the Art Deco buildings.

From Greenhill's central position, there is a multi-choice menu of excursions. Tour the many vineyards, or play on a spectacular golf course sited above the steep cliffs of Cape Kidnappers, a craggy coastal landscape that is also home to the world's largest most accessible gannet colony. On your return, your Greenhill hosts will welcome you back as if you were royalty.

Greenhill – The Lodge
Hawke's Bay
New Zealand
Tel: (64 6) 879-9944
Fax: (64 6) 879-9940
E-mail: enquiries@greenhill.co.nz
Internet: www.greenhill.co.nz

The Marlborough Sounds

New Vintage

Hotel d'Urville Blenheim, New Zealand

At the top of the South Island of New Zealand lie the sheltered blue waters of the spectacular Marlborough Sounds. This marine playground provides a perfect environment for water sports, from sailing and cruising to diving and sea kayaking. The myriad of peaceful bays and coves that make up the Sounds are home to blue dolphins, penguins, seals and native birds.

Not far from this water haven is the Hotel d'Urville. With its grand-columned frontage, this is a landmark building in the small town of Blenheim, center of the "new world" wine region of Marlborough. The hotel is named after renowned French explorer Dumont d'Urville, a brilliant, enigmatic sailor who made two great voyages to the Pacific as Commander of the ship *Astrolabe* in the 1800s. In search of a site for a French penal colony, he surveyed New Zealand, and charted the fjords of the Sounds, but was beaten by Britain to claiming the country for France.

However, 200 years later, there is a far more favorable connection with France than a prison would have been: French wine stock grows here, and Marlborough sauvignon blancs, such as the famous Cloudy Bay label, win awards and accolades in Europe and North America.

The bank vault lobby

The Havana Room's antique matching sleigh beds face a huge mirror that expands the narrow space. An old medicine cabinet and colonial copper milk cooler are decorative conversation pieces adding interest to this simple room.

This is one of the key viticultural regions of New Zealand, where the climate has been compared to Burgundy in France. Yet New Zealand's long narrow shape, which means that nowhere is more than 80 miles (130 km) from the sea, provides a unique maritime climate. Most of the vineyards are in coastal areas, warmed by day with clear sunlight and cooled by sea breezes at night.

In only 30 years since the first vineyard was established, Marlborough has become the largest wine-growing region in New Zealand. Some 30 or so wineries have been established, growing grape varieties such as sauvignon blanc, chardonnay, riesling and pinot gris. Red varieties such as pinot noir, cabernet sauvignon and merlot are also planted here. The soil types, abundant sunshine, long autumns and crisp, cool winters have proved the right ingredients to deliver world-class wines. Such is the quality of the *terroir* here that international wine companies have invested in the region, with Swiss, French and Australian labels staking out their own claims.

Built in the 1920s, the old bank building has been skilfully converted into a new use. The grand staircase leads guests upstairs to what was once a walk-in vault, and which now forms the central corridor that leads to the bedrooms. Now you can deposit yourself for safe keeping in this small nine-room hotel. The huge steel vault doors have been kept, complete with their original brass plaques and studs.

While the decoration is eclectic, this is not a euphemism for a mess. Themed rooms are a trend in many hotels, as proprietors strive to differentiate their establishment from others to appeal to the often-jaded palette of the regular traveler bored with the standard hotel room look. The themes here are understated, often more of a hint rather than fully realized, which is a more elegant interpretation.

The classic lines of the d'Urville Suite recall New Zealand's colonial days, with a nautical feel in the blue paneling to the dado line, a brass ship's bell, charts and antique maps. Drawings by the Astrolabe's resident artist line the walls.

A blaze of warm red enlivens the entrance to the Colours Room. Bold contrasts of high impact colors on the walls and fabrics are picked up by glass ornaments. This is a high-energy room with a relaxing atmosphere.

Downstairs is the d'Urville wine bar and brasserie, with its much praised menu and a young chef who uses the local produce and wines to full advantage, gaining the restaurant an international reputation. A patchwork of orchards and vineyards, Marlborough is described as New Zealand's gourmet's province, and is home to the famous green-lipped mussels, farmed salmon and locally grown olive oil. During the long, hot summer, guests can sit at tables in the open air surrounded by vines. And in winter, sampling the regional red wines in front of the fire in the bar is a welcome relaxation after a day on the slopes of the nearby ski fields.

With its agreeable (more than agreeable, actually) climate, the country's highest sunshine hours and an easygoing lifestyle focused on wine, food and water, Marlborough is a tourist magnet. And the whale-watching capital of the world, Kaikoura, is less than two hours' drive away for the biggest fish story of them all.

The Kuba Room is adorned with old African ceremonial textiles and tapestries. An old teak box displays small intricate carvings and colorful telephone wire baskets made by Ndebele women.

Hotel d'Urville

Blenheim
New Zealand

Tel: (64 3) 577-9945
Fax: (64 3) 577-9946
E-mail: hotel@durville.com
Internet: www.durville.com

Location, Location, Location

In a Russian version of Monopoly, the prime real estate on the board must be Red Square, the historic and political heart of Moscow. The huge square is a magnet for Russian and foreign visitors, its every side flanked by some of the city's most famous tourist attractions. History has been made and remade in this place.

Red Square's centerpiece is St. Basil's Cathedral, a fantastic conglomeration of domes, cupolas, arches, towers and spires; an architectural masterpiece unmatched for its sheer visual exuberance. Brightly and multicolored, it dominates the vast gray cobbled expanse before and around it. Tsar Ivan the Terrible commissioned the cathedral to commemorate a battle victory. Legend has it that on its completion in 1556, the aptly named tsar ordered that the architect be blinded so that he could not match or outdo its splendor in the future. Napoleon was apparently so impressed with St. Basil's he wanted to take it back to Paris. Fortunately that was impossible, so it stands here still, long after he tried to burn it down and Bolshevik- and Stalinist-era plots to demolish it were thwarted.

Most of Moscow's key sights are within five minutes' walk of Red Square, as is the imposing Le Royal Meridien National, definitely in the best position for visiting the city's attractions.

Le Royal Meridien National's main entrance

St. Basil's Cathedral

Le Royal Meridien National is part of **a very different Moscow** now, a city more outward looking and increasingly cosmopolitan as it experiences rapid social change.

Corner façade of Le Royal Meridien National

Majolica panel on the façade

Statues of the Atlantes flank
the hotel elevators

Lenin's Mausoleum is just minutes from here. The embalmed body of the founder of the Communist state is entombed in full view of where he once lived: Room 107 of Le Royal Meridien National. The bedroom he stayed in for a week in March 1918 was "decorated in tender pink shades." Lenin moved into the Kremlin as head of the Bolshevik Government; the National was renamed the First House of the Soviets. It became a convenient residence for Party officials for more than a decade, re-opening under its original name in 1932.

Famous and infamous guests have entered the impressive doors of the National since it first opened in 1903. Then, its comfort and luxury, and innovations such as electric elevators attracted much favorable attention. Royals to diplomats, politicians to priests, businessmen to academics, authors and artists; all have enjoyed the hotel's proximity to the Kremlin, the Bolshoi Theatre, museums and the like. Many of them are guests here forever, their photographs framed in the hotel portrait gallery.

Standing at the crossroads of Tverskaya and Mokhovaya streets, looking across the Alexandrovsky Gardens to the Kremlin and Red Square, the National has been a silent witness to many of the tumultuous events in Russian history. Prosperity, devastation, war and revolution have all visited here some time or other.

In the 1990s, after the collapse of the Soviet Union, the hotel underwent a major overhaul lasting some five years. Its stone façades were restored, the interiors made elegant again with antique furniture and art, restaurants suites and rooms updated, another floor added. Le Royal Meridien National is part of a very different Moscow now, a city more outward looking and increasingly cosmopolitan as it experiences rapid social change. Key figures in past and present Russian politics, Comrades Lenin and Stalin together with the current President Vladimir Putin, loiter near the National Historical Museum at the edge of Red Square, posing for paid photographs with tourists. Under the watchful eye of police, they are actor lookalikes, the first two a rather eerie reminder of sterner times, the latter an indication of an apparently more tolerant mood.

Moscow is loaded with architecture, museums and galleries. Now it has plenty of that major attraction, shopping. Most of the famous brands and several of the global retail chains are here, from clothes to restaurants. Capitalism rather than military might is on display, from the enterprising elderly strawberry sellers on the side of the motorway as we drove in from the airport, to the number of luxury cars seen on city roads and the myriad of souvenir stalls doing a brisk business in Soviet-era memorabilia. Many buildings are being renovated or are under construction. Cafés, clubs, casinos and cinemas beckon to the newly prosperous.

Bedroom of the Classic Suite

The antique-filled National Suite

The iconostasis in the Archangel's Cathedral

Over the weekend we visited, the inner city was crowded with people enjoying time off and out in the balmy summer weather. Contemporary life Western-style is very evident: teenagers texting on cell phones, fashionably dressed shoppers strolling the elegant arcades of GUM, the huge department store next to St. Basil's, and browsing in the malls. In the gardens, families picnicked and gathered at the ice-cream stands, children played in the fountains, people chatted in cafés. Brides were everywhere, blossoming like giant white flowers in the green garden and against the gray of Red Square. A group of armed soldiers marched past and then re-appeared, this time toting musical instruments. They began to play a catchy American tune, and dancing broke out at the ramparts of the Kremlin, couples waltzing and fox-trotting in the sun.

A stairway in the hotel

Muscovites and visitors alike were relaxing and enjoying the sights, set against the memory of a recent Communist era, one perhaps epitomized in Western minds by the Kremlin. In Russian, *kremlin* means "fortification" or "citadel," and it certainly presents as that. Centuries old, the Kremlin was the residence of the tsars, Bolshevik and Soviet rulers, now President Putin. A looming presence in the area, its red towers and yellow walls make a more cheerful color scheme than one might imagine for a place with rather grim Cold War–era associations. Above its high walls are tantalizing glimpses of gold domes, a hint of the stunning buildings only visible by going inside this bastion of power.

Domes of the Terem Palace

Inside, an architecturally diverse collection of buildings is testimony to an intriguing history. A tour of the Kremlin – although much is off-limits – reveals an ornate collection of ancient churches and palaces grouped among plainer government offices. Your entry ticket includes admittance to the superb Archangel's Cathedral, once the private church of the Russian grand dukes and tsars. Members of the ruling family were married here, infant heirs baptized, aristocratic confessions heard, and its burial vault their final resting place. Inside the chapels are precious frescoes and icons. Our visit coincided with a choir recital. The unaccompanied voices of the four singers were hauntingly beautiful, almost otherworldly; surely blessed sounds even if you are non-religious. Next door, the staggering wealth of the tsars is displayed in the Armoury, the oldest museum in Russia.

Moscow Underground

Cathedral of Christ the Saviour

The city above ground is fascinating, and so is the underground. The Moscow metro is surely the most decorative of the world's subways. Built to Stalin's orders and opened in 1935, the stations have been called "the people's palaces" because of their remarkable architecture and interior design. The lavish use of marble, mosaics, sculptures and chandeliers make the crowded stations almost sumptuous, and certainly dramatic. Dozens of bronze statues – soldiers, farmers, factory workers and students – decorate one stop; artful propaganda in this and many others illustrate, and embellish, Russia's Communist past.

Although now part of an international hotel group, the National is managed and staffed by Russians, so it has retained much of its local flavor. The cheerful commissionaires and charming concierges are an ever-helpful source of information. Moscow is a place you can quite easily spend a week visiting, and the National is an ideally located headquarters in this very walkable and colorful city.

Le Royal Meridien National
Moscow
Russian Federation

Tel: (7 495) 258-7000
Fax: (7 495) 258-7100
E-mail: hotel@national.ru
Internet: www.national.ru

Orientation

| Raffles Hotel | Singapore, Singapore |

"Immortalized by writers and patronized by everyone," said an anonymous journalist, about this classic hotel in the 1930s, when Singapore was known as the crossroads of the East and the Raffles label was seen on the steamer trunk of every seasoned traveler.

Built in 1887, it was declared a national monument by the Government a century later, and as can happen when governments take an interest in private property, it soon after closed down. However, this story has a happy ending, as the closure was for a major restoration. The hotel's first heyday was in 1915, and this date was used as the benchmark for returning Raffles to its elegant look of the times when sultans, statesmen, scribes and stars all tasted the colonial high life here.

This "White House" of Singapore, facing Beach Road and the South China Sea, is named after Sir Stamford Raffles, who founded modern Singapore in 1819. One of the few remaining great 19th-century hotels in Asia, Raffles has its own signature tune. The 1915 *Raffles March* was commissioned by the then proprietors of what was reported to be the "most magnificent establishment of its kind East of Suez." In addition, it has its own museum, a collection of travel memorabilia about itself, and its own drink, called the Singapore Sling, which is a complex concoction of gin, cherry brandy, cointreau, benedictine, pineapple juice, grenadine and a dash of Angostura bitters, more a fruit salad than a cocktail. An exotic taste, like the city of Singapore itself.

The neo-Renaissance façade of Raffles Hotel

The Sikh doorman

Orientation is, in zoological terms, the ability of animals to find their way back to a distant place, as in homing pigeons and migratory birds. Attracted to its history, I had stayed at Raffles a decade ago, definitely its shabby days. On my return, to see how it looked after its facelift, it had re-oriented itself to being a "Grand Historic Hotel of the Far East."

From the gleaming façade and the glamorous doorman to the resplendent lobby and lush gardens, this is a place transformed. All signs of shabbiness had been thoroughly dismissed, the hotel literally shone, every rough edge filed off and buffed to a gleam. This is a glittering comeback; a triumphant return after long and expensive cosmetic surgery with a new look that respects yet belies its real age. The original cast-iron portico that once sheltered the hotel entrance from tropical downpours, yet was removed in 1919, has been reconstructed complete with the original stained glass.

The lobby and its atrium attract crowds of visitors, so much so that it is closed mid-evening to all but the residents themselves. Each of the generously sized suites has its original 14-foot ceiling, arches and ceiling fans sustain the spacious airy atmosphere, and light filters in through the verandah windows. Floors are teak, marble and tile, and the elegant period furnishings and oriental carpets add character. The old wooden and brass switch plates make an attractive feature of a necessary fitting. Although the feel of bygone days has been preserved, the rooms are not museum-like.

"Feed at Raffles when visiting Singapore" was Rudyard Kipling's advice many years ago, and still relevant. The Raffles Grill and the Tiffin Room with its famous specialty, tiffin curry, are renewed classic fixtures. The Writers' Bar – where novelists and travel writers such as Joseph Conrad, Somerset Maugham and Noel Coward made notes and conversation – still serves your choice of planter's punch, as does the Long Bar, although this has moved its location and changed substantially from its original incarnation. A hotel legend centers on the Bar & Billiard Room, where in 1902 the last tiger to be shot in Singapore met its demise, actually under the building, not, as a more fanciful story would have it, under the billiard table.

The lobby and the original grand wooden staircase

Suite 361

Bathroom of suite 361

Now there are other restaurants to feed at, the Raffles Hotel Arcade adjoining the original building has many more, the Empress Room with its Cantonese cuisine an elegant choice. Or you could leave the hotel's tropical garden surroundings of palm trees, ferns and orchids to walk (literally) just around the corner to the Imperial Herbal restaurant for a consultation with the herb doctor. You may be prescribed a variety of Chinese dishes and liquids to balance your yin with your yang. With luck one will be the delicious braised eggplant with pine nuts, but other dishes are just as good. (Maybe not the deep-fried scorpions and crunchy black ants.)

In front of the hotel are several Singapore white plumerias. Often planted around Asian temples, this tropical tree with its fragrant white flowers has been honored by Buddhists for centuries as a symbol of immortality. The hardy plumeria is a continually flowering tree, a fitting match to the enduring legend that is Raffles.

The Somerset Maugham Suite

Raffles Hotel

Singapore
Singapore

Tel: (65) 337-1886
Fax: (65) 337-7650
E-mail: raffles@pacific.net.sg
Internet: www.singapore-raffles.raffles.com

Hotel Claris

Egyptology at the Claris

A Balanced Dynamic

| Hotel Claris | Barcelona, Spain |

On Spain's Costa Dorada, named for its golden sand beaches, is the Mediterranean seaport of Barcelona, the capital city of the Catalonian region.

Catalonia has a long and proud history of rebellion and independence. It was from here that Christopher Columbus set out on his voyage of discovery. Today it is deservedly famous for its collection of extraordinary buildings designed by Spain's most famous architect, Antoni Gaudí, during the early part of the 20th century, as well as architecture from the 15th century.

Even the airport is stylish, a fitting entry to this design-oriented city, which mixes medieval, Art Nouveau and modern architecture, and was home to great artists such as Pablo Picasso, Salvador Dalí and Joan Miró.

Behind the ornate 19th-century façade of Hotel Claris is yet another collection in this city of collections. The Claris has its own Egyptian museum on the mezzanine above the lobby, open only to guests. Here you can take tea and out-stare a small sphinx, inspect the mummies, statues and carvings and pretend to be a discovering archaeologist, all in the comfort of your own hotel.

The Claris foyer with mosaics and statues

The owner of the hotel has assembled this ancient collection. Senor Jordi Clos i Llombart is one of Spain's leading Egyptologists and the founder of Barcelona's Egyptology Museum, which houses the rest of his collection.

Behind the exterior of what was once a palace are cutting-edge interiors, balancing classicism and contemporary design, typical of Barcelona.

The Claris has an expansive lobby in which guests may watch the world go by. Here, ancient mosaic fragments and marble toga-clad Roman busts are juxtaposed with contemporary furniture by Oscar Tusquets. The hotel doorman, clad in white, is another chic trademark of the Claris.

Our room is reminiscent of a ship's cabin, and had parquet floors, kilim rugs and intriguing antique pieces, modern furniture and relics. But few sailors would be used to rich colors of russet wood and purple and room to move on two levels, all of which make this such a stylish space. And the closest expanse of water is the generously sized open-air swimming pool up on the hotel roof, where a city-center panoramic view is a bonus.

Hotel Claris is in the heart of metropolitan Barcelona, only a street away from the most fashionable and gracious avenue in the city, the Paseo de Gracia. On this broad and tree-lined street are two of Gaudí's most admired and visited buildings – the Casa Batlló and the Casa Milá (known as La Pedrera, the Quarry). It is worth the climb up to the Casa Milá's amazing roof, topped with giant surreal superstructures – chimneys and ventilation shafts said to have inspired Darth Vader's helmet!

These are but two of Gaudí's bizarre and brilliant buildings, which are often likened to massive sculptures. While highly original, his forms are functional – the free-form architecture reflecting his belief in providing natural methods of ventilation. Curved lines in the interiors, incorporation of the outdoors, and living spaces with moveable walls are trademarks of this creative architect's unique work. Now recognized as a visionary, Gaudí's ideas are compatible with modern architectural thought and the growing acceptance of the benefits of "biological living."

A mecca for admirers of Modernism, Barcelona has Europe's greatest collection of Art Nouveau buildings. Although the movement inspired him, Gaudí's interpretation was unique. A soaring sight on the city skyline is the spectacular sandcastle spires of his Church of the Sagrada Familia. Only one filigree stone tower was complete when Gaudí died in 1926, but work continues, a hundred years since it was begun, on this evolving organic artwork. In the manner of the great medieval cathedrals, his church is still not finished.

After marvelling at the Gaudí buildings close to the Claris, sit at the bar of the nearby Replay café, drink coffee

and watch the parade of passing Barcelonans. Or visit the design store of Vincón, with everything stylish for the home from fabrics to furniture.

Barcelona's most famous street, La Rambla, is an amble from the Paseo de Gracia. The busy promenade leading down to the waterfront is edged with cafés and bars, dotted with seats, trees and newsstands. Its mass of flower stalls color and perfume the length of the street. La Rambla continues to the Columbus monument honoring the Catalan discoverer of the New World.

Suite at the Claris

241

Rooftop pool at the Claris

Storefront on Rambla Avenue

Barcelona is considered Spain's culinary capital, and it's here you will find one of the most spectacular food markets. Mercat de la Boqueria has been the central market in the Rambla area for more than 160 years. Ornate iron columns, buttresses and arches support a large covered pavilion, underneath which are the 500 or so food stalls. Few of the market's original Art Nouveau stalls and fixtures are left, the most famous is Ramona's. With its bright stained-glass signs, cast iron columns and mosaic tiled sides, it attracts many admirers.

A xuxo, a fluffy cream-filled type of croissant sprinkled with sugar, is a delicious breakfast. You can walk the damage off, checking out the cheeses, wines, meats and fish. By now you may be ready to try a tortilla while appraising mushrooms, olives, herbs, salad greens ... Then take a rest from this gastronomic onslaught at one of the tapas bars, with a glass of cava, the Catalan sparkling wine.

Another of Barcelona's treasured collections is the paintings of Picasso. The Museu Picasso is in the medieval Barri Gòtic (Gothic Quarter), with its warren of streets and plazas one of the city's most interesting neighborhoods.

The Casa Batlló, façade designed by Antoni Gaudí in 1904, with its "dragon-back" roof of green ceramic tile

Luckily, to enjoy all this and more, the days seem to last longer. That may be because meals are later – lunch between 1 and 3 p.m., dinner around 9 or 10 p.m. The late nights can be spent in the many designer bars and clubs.

For a restful daytime experience, spend time in the gardens of the Park Güell. Take a picnic, sit on the mosaic tiled benches on the great serpentine curving terrace and admire the ornamented pavilions of another inventive and original Gaudí legacy to this fortunate city.

Hotel Claris
Barcelona
Spain
Tel: (34 3) 487 62 62
Fax: (34 3) 487 54 43
Email: claris@clerbyhotels.com
Internet: www.hotelclaris.com

Puppy Love

Gran Hotel Domine / Bilbao, Spain

In the old Spanish city of Bilbao, with a history of shipbuilding and seagoing, the Guggenheim Museum rises from the side of the Nervion riverbank like some fantastic creature of the deep, sunning itself out of the water. It is guarded on the street side by its own dog, a playful, flower-decked, 33 foot (10 m) high "puppy" that is likely the most humorous artwork ever done by Jeff Koons. With a coat of many colors, festooned with marguerite daisies, vivid marigolds and multicolored impatiens, it is appealing both for its sillyness and its odd contrast with the massive sculpture that it sits so perkily in front of.

Described by its architect, Frank Gehry, as a shipwreck and by others as a whale, the Museum is permanently beached in this Basque city, now basking in the ownership of one of the world's most astonishing buildings. The exterior rewards the gaze at all times of the day and night, from many angles. Its titanium surface reflects the changing light and color of the sky, offering a constantly varying spectacle.

Just a few doors down from the puppy, literally across the road from this fabulous draw, is the contemporary Gran Hotel Domine. Its mirrored façade reflects its dynamic neighbor, and its rooms offer a full-frame, unimpeded view of the monumental museum.

Inspired by the proximity to the Guggenheim, the hotel's local architect Inaki Aurrecoetxea has designed a building frontage that looks to have eyelids, all the better to see the view beyond. Inside, the interior designers have chosen to show off some of the 20th century's best design work, from art to furniture. However, form does not triumph over function; this may be contemporary design but it is comfortable and usable. The interior design elements, from hotel uniforms to light fixtures have all been chosen or overseen by Javier Mariscal, whose playful personality shines through in much of the hotel. He would approve of toddler George using the very stylish Moroso banquette seat as a playground.

The public spaces in this designer hotel are sleek but welcoming, open to the locals as well as guests. The foyer is often alive with people, satisfying the hotel's intention that there be "always something going on" and that it be part of Bilbao society. Key entertaining events like weddings and birthday parties are held here, the bars and cafés obviously popular, with a parade of people interestingly dressed in the latest Spanish fashions or streetwear. The top-level terrace is also an observation deck that brings you level with the top of the Gehry structure. The generous breakfast served up here has a tempting range of local specialties: little pots of rice pudding, frittata, olive and tomato bread add to the usual fare.

Boy meets banquette

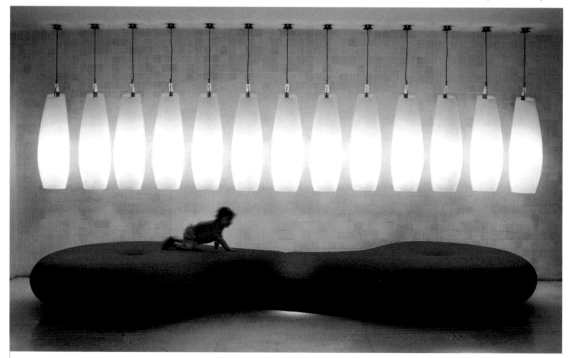

Reception and *Cypress Fossil*

Guest rooms are simply designed and luxuriously decked out, again with "name" furniture and fixtures, from the Starck bathtub to the Alvar Aalto stool. A glass wall separates and links the bedroom with the bathroom, and ensures the view extends throughout the room. At night, as well as chocolates, playthings appear on each pillow; a designer black squeaky toy, something different decided by Mariscal that is appealing even for grown-ups, many of whom ask for a matching set or more for their children (supposedly). A cat, dog or sheep arrives in the room every night you are there.

The atrium of the hotel features a massive Mariscal artwork. The *Cypress Fossil* sculpture assembles 90 tons of stones, stacked and wrapped in delicate wire mesh and looks like some huge deep-sea fishing net suspended from the sky. It reaches up from the ground floor to the terrace skylight and creates a startling inner landscape.

... form does not triumph over function; this may be contemporary design but it is comfortable and usable.

Splash & Crash Bar

A suite

The influx of tourists, dominated by building-watchers who come to visit this still-new Mecca for museums, has led to a burst of "accessory building." A soaring bridge, with night-lighted floor, curves across the river like a masted ship. A stunning design by prolific Spanish architect Santiago Calatrava, this footbridge is one more architectural pleasure to look at and walk over. The new underground, with its clear crustacean-like entrances popping up in the wide streets and squares is like another subterranean creature revealing a curve of its back. Designed by British architect Sir Norman Foster, and affectionately dubbed by the locals as Fosteritos, the entrances look rather like a gigantic slinky toy. The clear glass entrance sheds light down the escalators so that the descent seems less of a journey down into darkness than in most other underground systems.

It has been said that the city itself is not worth visiting other than for the Guggenheim. Not so — it has enough personality to warrant more than a brief excursion to the museum alone. Bilbao's Old Town – Casco Viejo – is a medieval quarter full of cafés and bars along its dark shadowy crisscrossing streets, with Gothic façaded buildings and a hidden central square. The Plaza Nueva has a Sunday market for hundreds of singing birds, the canaries matching the color of the buildings. Stamps, coins, flowers and a miscellany of junk is for sale. Atmospheric bars and cafés dot the perimeter, with Casa Victor Montes and Victor being the best choices. Nearby, the La Ribera food market is in a stunning domed building with rich stained-glass windows. A great variety of fish, meat and vegetables are laid out on every counter, like still-life works of art.

The Zubi Zuri footbridge

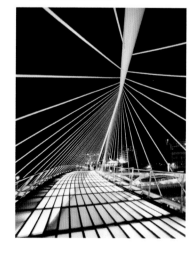

The Guggenheim Bilbao Museum

Basque cuisine is often hailed as Spain's best. *Pintxos* are the Basque version of tapas, a great variety of appetizers arranged on the bar counter. We snacked rather than dined, and you can walk and eat with delicious takeout from the many bakeries and patisseries. *Bacalao* is a local speciality, cod more classically cooked in garlic and olive oil with red peppers, but on every menu in many different guises. The local fruity white wine is Txakoli, and there are plenty of reds to choose from, the classic being rioja, together with cava, the Spanish sparkling wine and Spanish beers.

Great shopping is available, in the museum, along the Gran Via de Don Diego, the main avenue, and in the Old Town. The hotel, too, has a variety of Mariscal-designed gifts, for yourself or others. In the Gran Hotel Domine brochure it says that it wants to be a place that appeals to business executives who miss their homes, as well as travelers who are escaping theirs. Both will be content here.

Gran Hotel Domine
Bilbao
Spain
Tel: (34 4) 944 253 300
Fax: (34 4) 944 253 301
E-mail: ghdb@granhoteldominebilbao.com
Internet: www.granhoteldominebilbao.com

ICEHOTEL at night, with the Aurora Borealis

In the Hall of the Mountain King

ICEHOTEL / Jukkasjärvi, Sweden

Some 20 miles (32 km) inside the Arctic Circle, the temperature –13°F (–25°C), Lapland is no place for fashion victims. Here you wear the clothes the hotel has determined are right for the conditions – at least the outer garments. When you feel just how cold it is here, you'll be happy to climb into the Michelin-man insulation suits and the fur hats provided.

ICEHOTEL is in Swedish Lapland, in the small village of Jukkasjärvi, in the heart of reindeer-herding territory. It takes two hours or so to fly from Stockholm to the airport of Kiruna. There you choose to be met by the hotel shuttle bus for the 10-minute ride to Jukkasjärvi or a Husky-drawn sled for a two-hour transfer with a difference.

Rooms can be reserved only from November through to May – and even then only if it is cold enough. For this is a hotel that re-invents itself every year according to the weather. It depends on ice for both its form and its fame. Winter's onset dictates the building of the ICEHOTEL, while the arrival of spring heralds its self-destruction. The temperature warms up, the hotel melts down: the ultimate spring cleaning.

The biggest igloo in the world, ICEHOTEL is literally sculpted from nearby river ice. Building begins at the end of October, or during November, depending on weather conditions. It takes temperatures of 27°F (−3°C) and some six to eight weeks work to construct the shell. Snow cannons spray 30,000 tons of manufactured snow onto specially made metal molds. Once the snow is sufficiently hard, the molds are removed. As the exterior construction proceeds, the interior structure and decoration begins. Bearing walls and pillars, furniture and sculptures are made from huge cylindrical iceblocks cut out from the frozen river with a special ice saw. By mid-January, cold permitting, the building is completed.

The result is a hotel that can accommodate 100 people, and which includes a bar, cinema and chapel. The stunning entrance hall is an arched cavern with a snow ceiling and windows of translucent iceblocks. Because the river is slow running, the ice freezes with few air bubbles and the density gives it a distinct blue glow. This colonnade of ice is complete with a grand chandelier, made entirely of ice, and lit with optical fibers.

The entrance hall

A bedroom, chill factor 23°F (–5°C)

Every year the hotel takes on a different design. The annual rebuilding gives the hotel designers opportunity to refine their ideas, and increase their "snow-how." Local ice sculptors add their work to the interior, carving out a variety of whimsical pieces, from bears and Huskies to ice televisions and fans.

Entering the grand reception hall is to arrive in another realm, an ice palace where a glittering crystal power rules supreme. The King of Cold's stern domain is white, sparkling clear and majestically lit with a mass of candles. The omnipresent silence inside that pervades this cool chamber invites whispers rather than normal speech. After the fiercely chilling outside air it feels positively warm, even though it is only approximately 23°F (–5°C).

Having greeted us warmly at the frozen reception desk, our igloo guide Thor points out that few guests lounge around in the lobby to people-watch. That's not surprising – the seats are actually ice blocks covered with reindeer skins.

All the furniture in the hotel is made of ice – and that includes the beds, also blanketed with reindeer skins. The choice of rooms ranges from standard through to suites, usually more richly decorated. Rooms are made individual by artworks and sculptures, although ice is common to all. White linen curtains serve for bedroom doors. There are no heaters or hairdryers, or even bathrooms – these are located in another building.

On the night we stayed, the in-house movie theater (with ice bench seats, upholstered in fur) screened the latest Batman movie with Arnold Schwarzenegger as the evil Iceman. In this climate the audience related more to the villain than the hero.

The hotel bar is open to guests and visitors. But lean too long on this bar and you'll be a permanent fixture. The Absolut Vodka company is a partner in ICEHOTEL, and its brand is inevitably the only vodka available. The other product placement is at the bar entrance; the opening is cut in the distinctive shape of the Absolut Vodka bottle. Beer is off the menu, as its low alcohol content means it would freeze in the cool atmosphere.

ICEHOTEL during the day

Road sign

A post-nuptial party was held in the bar after a wedding celebrated in the beautiful ice chapel, where the seats as well as the bride were clad in fur. The wedding photographs gave the phrase "freeze-frame" a new meaning. The newlyweds spent the first night of their honeymoon in the ice bridal suite. There are double sleeping bags.

On that same night guests were treated to an amazing bonus – the eerily beautiful spectacle of the Aurora Borealis. This luminous atmospheric phenomenon is triggered when particles from the sun collide with the earth's magnetic field. Here it is called the Northern Lights, and streaks of yellow, green, crimson and rose are painted across the starry Arctic sky as if some celestial artist is at work.

When it is time to chill out, guests are zipped into specially made Arctic survival sleeping bags designed to withstand temperatures down to –22°F (–30°C). The warm underlayers you are sensibly wearing are kept on, and your outer clothes stay snug in the sleeping bag with you. During the pre-retirement briefing, the guide advises sleeping on your back to avoid the possibility of your face freezing to the sleeping bag.

Lying in an all-white ice bedroom, surrounded by a total and deep quiet, flickering shadows thrown by the flickering candlelight, is like being inside a snow cave deep within a mountain. The room temperature varies between 25°F to 16°F (–4°C to –9°C), depending on how cold it is outside and the number of overnight guests – and you pay for this experience! Surprisingly, many say they slept soundly and warmly throughout the night.

Certificate of Coldworthiness

In the morning you are woken with room service bearing hot berry juice. A traditional sauna lures, authenticated by the Swedish Sauna Academy, whose motto is *in sauna veritas* – "in the sauna, truth is revealed." Now that you are conditioned to the chill factor, the steamy heat can come as a bit of a shock.

With a reconditioned thermostat, you can head to a generous Scandinavian breakfast in the restaurant across the road. The cold air heightens the appetite for cuisine from the Lapland pantry: game, berries, local venison and fish such as Arctic char.

The overnight experience can be extended with a stay in nearby wooden chalets, with full-tilt central heating. Daytime activities include safaris, with a team of 10 to 12 Huskies leading each expedition. There are more dogs than people in Jukkasjärvi. More than 900 sled dogs – Siberian and Alaskan Huskies – are ready to take you on a fast trip through the Laplandic landscape of frozen lakes and snow-dressed pine forests.

Impatient to be off, the dogs bark furiously while waiting. Once they start pulling their load, they are contentedly quiet, and all that can be heard is their padding feet and the sound of the sled gliding across the snow.

Parking outside ICEHOTEL is for snowbikes rather than the usual cars. The bikes cover the icy ground more efficiently than any car, although the chill factor is vastly greater. Kicksleds are another mode of transport seen in the parking lot. This is a sort of wooden chair on metal runners, propelled like a scooter. Driving lessons quickly qualify drivers for both snowbikes and kicksleds, which can be used for short trips or longer expeditions to wilderness camps.

Husky team transfer sled to the airport

First built in 1990, ICEHOTEL has been a successful venture. Last year, nearly 4,000 guests stayed overnight, while 20,000 day visitors saw the massive snow and ice sculpture and enjoyed the adventure activities offered in this stunning spot on top of the world.

Adventurers staying over in ICEHOTEL are presented with a certificate on their departure, as a permanent reminder of their igloo experience. They may have been comforted to know that the Cold Center, specialists in sub-zero physiology, was close at hand, in nearby Kiruna.

ICEHOTEL
Jukkasjärvi
Sweden
Tel: (46 980) 66800
Fax: (46 980) 66890
E-mail: reception@jukkas.se
Internet: www.jukkas.se

Goreme in the distance, bathed in evening light

Caving in Cappadocia

| Esbelli Evi House | Urgūp Turkey |

Millions of years ago volcanic eruptions and the forces of erosion sculpted a fanciful and extraordinary sandstone landscape in the remote valleys of Cappadocia, in central Turkey. Humans have added to these outlandish and amazing natural forms over the centuries, carving houses, hermit cells, churches, catacombs and underground cities from the soft rock and pinnacles.

Driving down into the village of Urgūp, we're struck by the blending of landscape and buildings. Color and shape merge to such a degree it is almost impossible to tell where the village begins and ends. From a distance, the houses appear to melt into the pale gold rock of the cliffs. Located at the edge of Urgūp and nestled against low cliffs is Esbelli Evi House, a restored cave pension. The bedrooms are probably the oldest in the hotel business, as they date back to the sixth century, while the upper building was added in the 18th century. The upper floor's reception and reading room are decorated with antique Turkish rugs and low brass tables, classic and elegant. Downstairs, the bedrooms are a labyrinth of caves hollowed out from the hillside's soft rock. The smooth honey-colored stone of the walls is both cool and atmospheric. These cave rooms are simply furnished with kilim rugs, antique brass beds and some include a fireplace.

Esbelli Evi House at night

Bought and converted into a guesthouse a decade ago by owner Suha Ersov, Esbelli Evi House is easily the most interesting hotel in the area. Of the eight bedrooms, one was originally a kitchen, another a stable and a third a wine pressing room. Suha prefers to run Esbelli Evi as a house rather than a hotel. He shows his guests the sitting room, stocked with an eclectic range of books, CDs and chess sets, the kitchen with its well-stocked refrigerator, and a do-it-yourself laundry, and tells them to make themselves at home.

Classic kilim rugs on the stone floors belonged to Suha's grandmother, and his mother made the traditional lace curtains, enhancing the feeling of being in a private home. Like home, there is no restaurant or room service, but the breakfast room on the rooftop patio serves tasty breads, hard-boiled eggs, fruit and coffee. Sitting in the morning sun drinking coffee and looking out over the village and mountains beyond seems a valid activity for quite some time. For lunch or dinner, village restaurants just a stroll down the hill serve excellent local food and wine. A short drive from Esbelli Evi House are the Gulludere and Kizilcukur Valleys, known as the Red and Rose Valleys. These are a fantasy of pink sandstone shapes and erosion-formed gullies that glow orange and red at sunset, attracting busloads of tourists in the busy season to watch from the vantagepoint of the parking areas. The valleys are a stunning sight, better viewed without a horde of onlookers, but worth seeing whenever.

Reception and reading room

In this spectacular landscape, hundreds of cone-shape rock forms have been gouged out over the centuries to serve as crude living accommodations, stables or churches. Doors and windows are often dozens of feet from the ground. On the valley's lower path, Ayvali Kilise (the Church of the Quince) is a cave church with wonderful interior wall paintings dating from the 11th century. Scattered about this stone wonderland are occasional vineyards and orchards where a farmer or two may be seen toiling away behind a horse-drawn plow. No television aerials or telephone poles intrude on a walk through this timeless landscape. Along the track we find a café carved in the rock, with log seats to enjoy Turkish coffee.

Rock houses at Uchisar

The Kitchen Room cave bedroom, once an old kitchen, the oven now the wardrobe

Several miles away we drive through the village of Uchisar, where colorful roadside market stalls lie at the foot of a cluster of towering rock houses typical of the area. Still further on, we stop to look over the village of Goreme. The vista is a dazzling array of rock formations, the architecture mixing recent conventional rock buildings with ancient conical houses and churches. All are aglow in the golden evening light. In the distance, the call to prayer breaks the deep silence, adding an eerie soundtrack to an already fantastical scene.

The following day we are to go hot-air ballooning, our first experience of this mode of flight. Owned, operated and piloted by husband and wife Lars-Eric More and Kaili Kidner, the Kapadokya Balloon Company flies two hot-air balloons from April to November. This excursion means a very early morning wakeup call to first confirm that the weather is right. The day dawns stunning and perfect for flying with gas. On our arrival at 5:30 a.m., the balloons are inflated. Within minutes we are airborne ascending quietly into the warm early-morning light, standing in our cane basket lined with the local kilim carpet. As we climb, the sunrise etches long shadows into the amazing landscape. At 2,000 feet (610 m) I can appreciate the phrase "putting all your eggs in one basket." Feeling the breeze on your face as fresh air rather than a draft from aircraft air-conditioning is far more pleasant, though you do feel a deal more fragile.

Our last moments in
Turkey were happy ones,
as we discovered
Istanbul airport has
**a massive free tasting
counter of Turkish delight**,
in every flavor.

But we feel in capable hands, with our pilot in the same basket and happy to answer questions as she adjusts the burner above our head, and communicates with the other balloon and the ground crew. We descend to a few feet above the ground and pass so close to a group of apricot trees it is almost possible to reach out and pick the fruit before drifting lazily, dreamily up across the sky ... Of course landing is a key issue of ballooning – what goes up must come down is a very apt saying, and there's no coming in for another try. The pilot has to get it right the first time. We are impressed by the perfect touchdown, the basket bypassing bumpy fields to drop neatly upright on the back of the Jeep's trailer. When I congratulate the pilot on the faultless landing, she admits it is the first time she has achieved a direct hit onto the trailer. Once down, the balloons are packed away by the ground crew while the passengers are treated to cherry juice, champagne and cake to celebrate the flight. "Ballooning is one of the most beautiful things you can do in your life," Suha had told us. We agree – flying over the stunning lunar-like landscape of Cappadocia on such a magnificent morning has added to an unforgettable experience.

Room 16, cave bedroom with fireplace

Kapadokya Balloons, Goreme

Esbelli Evi House

Urgüp
Turkey

Tel: (90 384) 341-3395
Fax: (90 384) 341-8848
E-mail: suha@esbelli.com.tr
Internet: www.esbelli.com.tr

Circus Circus

Las Vegas, United States

Roll up, roll up, to the Biggest Show on Earth … An astounding 30.5 million people visit Las Vegas every year to see the constant spectacle of this town built on chance. The performance is the clash of the Titans come true, a showdown among mega-hotels competing for attention.

A glittering mecca for tourists, Las Vegas is now more of an entertainment than a gambling destination. Although you can gamble even at the airport, people come here more for the performance than for the casinos, which are now common in most American cities. For Las Vegas casino-resort owners, this means expanding what they offer to attract and keep customers within the walls of their hotels once they get there.

The glass pyramid of the Luxor Hotel, with Sphinx

Inside the Luxor; reception to the left – with an appropriately named shop for kids: Tiny Tuts

Is it a hotel or a city? The size of the Luxor Hotel is such that guests need maps. Ours covered just one side of this black glass pyramid with its 4,476 rooms. Las Vegas claims to have 19 of the world's 20 biggest hotels. The Bellagio, with 3,025 rooms is small by the city's standards – the MGM Grand has 5,005. In total there are around 120,000 rooms for rent.

Las Vegas is America's fastest growing city. Some 6,000 people move here every month – these include aspiring performers in search of employment in the ever-multiplying hotel casinos, or families and retirees looking for a place in the sun. Every one of them are attracted by the benign weather, bright lights, low taxes and affordable housing.

By day, the urban landscape is a strangely dull one. But come sundown, it is etched in neon and lights, and then it's showtime! Day and night, Las Vegas has a streetscape made up almost entirely of other cities' skylines: New York, Gaza's pyramid (just one), Paris with the Eiffel Tower, Venice with canals and gondolas, Bellagio with Lake Como.

America's images and icons increasingly colonize the world; now it seems that it is taking something of other countries back – souvenirs on a grand scale. Is a Museum of the World being created here, a world in miniature, where Americans, at least, don't need passports and travelers' checks? Here is Pocket Paris, Pocket New York and Pocket Venice, in scale and most of the key sights conveniently packaged close together for a concentrated and convenient visit. The city is a cheerful pastiche, with copies and caricatures of famous landmarks from around the world, sanitized and resized.

New York, New York; the tallest hotel, of course, recreates most of that city's famous landmarks: the Manhattan skyline with the Empire State and Chrysler buildings, Brooklyn Bridge, Times Square and the Statue of Liberty. Central Park is the casino's setting. The Manhattan Express is the world's first "heartline" twist-and-dive roller coaster.

Treasure Island, home of the mock sea battle between two galleons, one crewed by British imperialists, the other by American buccaneers. The British captain goes down with his ship – and both pop up a few minutes later, ready for the next performance.

Conspicuous consumption is everywhere, from the bargain all-you-can-eat buffets to energy-gobbling night-light extravaganzas. To some it is a display of conspicuous waste, one example being the destruction of old hotels to build new ones. You can see a video of the "implosion" of the old Aladdin Hotel on the website of the new Aladdin.

It's hard to see everything clamoring for your attention here. The tackiness is almost endearing in this show-off town which, like a kid, is out to impress – look at me, no me, HEY, ME!

Vegas caters both to the masses and to the elite; with a diverse range of entertainment, from pirate-themed Treasure Island, magicians and tiger tamers Siegfried and Roy to artists such as Van Gogh and Monet, "now appearing" at the Bellagio Art Gallery. Shopping, wedding chapels, the

The Bellagio and its fountains that dance to music

Liberace Museum and a museum for old neon signs also draw the crowds. When visitor numbers peak on weekends, so too do hotel room prices.

This is the experience economy at its zenith, where the artificial is accepted as natural: dancing fountains, erupting volcanos, the captain going down with his ship every hour on the hour after dusk; and Atlantis destroyed hourly in a nine-minute apocalypse. Open 24/7, this is Vegas Mean Time, where sunrise and sunset occur at 60-minute intervals in Caesar's Palace at the Forum.

You can boldly go where no one has gone before at the Star Trek Enterprise in the Las Vegas Hilton. This was the best casino styling, in keeping with the space theme. The warp-speed concept seems very appropriate to Vegas, home of virtual reality. Or explore the Pharaoh's tomb, without the heat and flies, at the Luxor.

Geographically themed hotels continue to open. Paris Vegas is to have a 50-storey tall, half-size replica of the Eiffel Tower, complete with restaurant partway up and a top floor viewing platform. Other faux French landmarks include the Paris Opera, the Louvre, the Arc de Triomphe and the Hôtel de Ville. Inside the casino a replica of the Pont Alexander III bridge will overlook shops and lead to the Eiffel Tower elevators. Eight French-inspired restaurants will include Le Pool Café; and Le Village Buffet. Le Casino will be très grand of course, with cobblestone paths and a 40-foot ceiling mural painted to look like the Parisian sky.

Costing US$1.6 billion, The Bellagio is the most expensive hotel ever built. It features a $300 million art collection, and branches of Tiffany, Armani and Prada. One of the few hotels that look good during the daylight hours, it is themed on Italy's Lake Como and the shoreside town of Bellagio. Italianate buildings with balustraded terraces surround a quarter-mile long artificial lake, to create an authentic atmosphere (except for the 36-storey hotel looming up behind and its syncopated fountains leaping high into the air). The Venetian, with its Piazza San Marco, a 315 foot (96 m) high reproduction of the Campanile and arched bridges, has gondoliers to row you on the canal winding through the shopping mall.

The Excalibur, home to the Round Table Buffet, Sir Galahad's RibRoom, and King Arthur's Tournament.

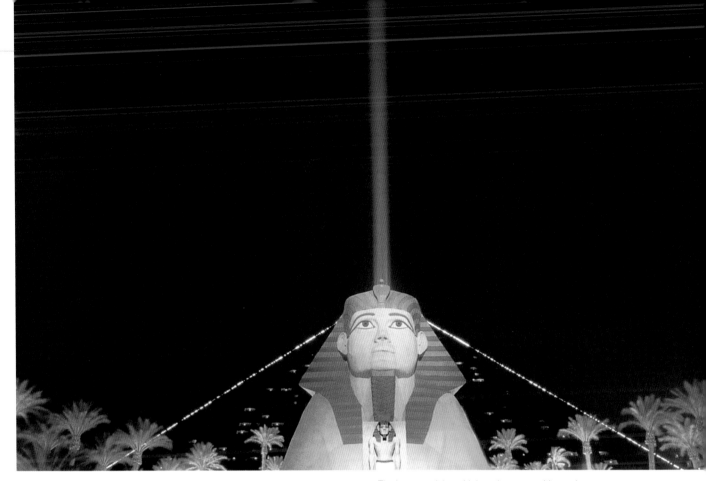

The Luxor at night, with laser beam to guide you home

In a town where spectacle is everything, and more of it arriving by the minute, the old Peggy Lee song *Is That All There Is?* comes to mind. With such sensory overload, it may well be true that excitement can become boring through repetition. Here high-rolling resort hotels are bidding to outperform their rivals. Vegas hoteliers must be performers and ringmasters in this Entertainment Capital of the World, where all the hotels are in show business.

Vegas on the Internet:

www.visitlasvegas.com
www.vegaslounge.com
www.vegas.com
www.lasvegaslife.com

Star Attraction

Avalon Hotel   Los Angeles, United States

Los Angeles: where the line between reality and unreality is deliberately blurred, much like the city view usually is, filtered through a smog haze typical of such megalopoli. Seen from the Getty Center, downtown L.A. has a surprisingly small number of high-rise buildings for a city that is famous for reaching for the stars.

Most of the "action, cut, take two or that's a wrap" variety in this tinsel-town – whose global image has been glamorously airbrushed by its megawatt movie industry and television series like *Baywatch* – is focused in the more low-rise parts of the city: the neighborhoods of Hollywood and Beverly Hills, where the California modern Avalon Hotel is located.

This is a small hotel that is more of a supporting actor than a big star, and so less demanding for that. More glamorous, glitzy and power-lunch dining rooms are elsewhere, with correspondingly bigger rooms and rates, but the Avalon is still a little gem. Subtle, understated and quietly settled in a residential neighborhood within walking distance of Rodeo Drive, it has low-key glamour – almost old-fashioned in its restraint. Even its signage is discreet, not writ large, just a clue that it is there rather than a shout. Polite notices at the subtly screened entrance ask departing guests to respect the neighbors' right to quiet.

L.A. viewed from the hilltop cactus garden of the Getty Center

The Avalon pool

The stunning hour-glass-shaped pool is a magnet, much less for swimmers, more as a chic place to meet for business or pleasure. Out on the sunny private patio that surrounds it, there are people surfing on laptops, talking on cell phones, in meetings, networking or just relaxing after work with friends. After five, it feels like it is a home away from home for those who live nearby in apartments; this is probably their local, providing surrogate outdoor space. The pool is the core of Avalon's mid-century style. Its shapely outline would have suited the curves of some of its most famous guests – Marilyn Monroe was once a resident, as was Mae West.

The reception

This is a bar and restaurant that happens to have a pool as its central focus, hence the name: *blue on blue*. The theme colors are water-focused; even the cocktails match; ask for a Moody Tuesday. The bar is known for its one-of-a-kind cocktail menu. Original Werner Panton designed metal chairs with teal velvet seats are among the covetable dining room furniture; other sleek vintage furniture icons and ceramics echo the 50s feel of the overall design.

The waterside cabanas with their citrus walls gives some tartness to the blue, sage green and white color scheme around the 50s vintage pool. Should you not want to be seen, you can privatize your cabana for a no-view by simply drawing the curtains across. These outdoor/indoor rooms are furnished with cushioned banquettes, tables, shag-pile rugs and candlelight: a swish California version of poolside dining.

Rooms in the Avalon's main building and neighboring apartment buildings, also 1950s-era, are stylish and laced with mid-century furnishings too. The latest technology is smoothly integrated, and room service is the expected contemporary 24/7 standard. Many have balconies that overlook the pool party scene below, good for discreet people-watching.

The basket-weave façade of the Avalon Hotel

Room with a view

The celebrity quotient is high in this part of town. You may glimpse some stars of the big and small screen shopping or dining. If not in the flesh, you might see eerily realistic mannequins in a store window; instantly recognizable models of real people making a behind-glass appearance wearing the same dress as the headless clotheshorse in front of them.

Shopping and eating fans are expertly indulged in Beverly Hills; upscale big brand stores, small boutiques and every kind of restaurant line the nearby streets. Jack & Jill's, an all-day breakfast café, is a surprisingly favorite stop for many locals. Its nostalgic down-home décor is inspired by farmhouse design. Hearty farmer-sized portions are served, although the diet-conscious can vary the ingredients according to their calorie plan.

The hip local Barneys department store buzzes with keen shoppers. The ground floor is a place of pilgrimage for Manolo Blahnik shoe aficionados; the top floor is the location of a stylish hard-to-find café (it is behind the shirt wall in the men's department). It has an outdoor terrace, with a good view and an all-day breakfast menu. Signature smoked fish is flown in daily from New York, and the delivery probably includes a top-up of New York "attitude" for the waiters.

Dining room detail

Window shopping

Stand-ins in-store

Bibliophiles should head to the Taschen bookstore on Beverly Drive. Its glamorous Philippe Starck interior is a showcase for the huge selection of books on art and popular culture. For art and culture under one very large roof, head to the Getty Center, the Richard Meier–designed building high up in the hills. This is an impressively well-organized place to visit, and you could easily spend a full day here, inside at the exhibitions and out in the gardens. If you are in search of the greater outdoors, Runyon Canyon, Sunset Ranch or Zuma Beach are all nearby.

If you'd rather stay "at home," indoor and outdoors are stylishly combined at the Avalon, a stylish urban retreat that is a star in a town full of them: the real and the dreamers.

Avalon Hotel
Los Angeles
United States
Tel: (310) 277-5221
Fax: (310) 277-4928

The Cardozo Hotel at twilight

Salsa City

| The Cardozo Hotel | Miami, United States |

The Cardozo Hotel looks like a sleek 1930s luxury liner moored on Ocean Drive. This masterpiece of streamlined design is a jewel among the many Art Deco gems on show in South Beach, part of the steamy tropical city of Miami.

Ocean Drive is a much-photographed streetscape of white and bright-colored buildings pictured against the clear blue skies, aquamarine sea and lush palm trees of a town that is hot in winter, and hotter in summer. South Beach offers sun, sand, sensuality, salsa and sizzling heat, a potent cocktail that attracts visitors to what is often called the American Riviera and the sexiest city in the States.

Built in 1939 and one of many buildings designed by the prolific architect Henry Hohauser, the Cardozo was once a retirement home, as were other hotels in South Beach. Now Gloria and Emilio Estefan, the Cuban-born superstar singer and her award-winning songwriter-musician husband own it. Their business empire markets Cuban culture on the American mainland, and the informal headquarters of Estefan Enterprises is the hotel's patio restaurant.

Reception with Marcus

With its white aerodynamic chairs, the Cardozo's beachfront lobby is reminiscent of a chic upper deck on a cruise ship. Just refitted, its original fireplace with marble mantel has been preserved, but in this climate it is for show rather than a necessity. The lobby's leopardskin patterned carpet is taken up for dancing to Latin bands on Thursday, Friday and Saturday nights, often until the sun comes up.

You can perch on a high stool at the glamorous mirrored bar, or sit on the porch with a martini and watch the world go by.

Overlooking the ocean, the upstairs rooms respond to the tropical environment with shutters to close out the bright afternoon light for a siesta, old style planters' chairs to lounge around in and a languorous atmosphere redolent of sultry climes.

The Cardozo, and South Beach, market romance and relaxation, delivering on their promise in a winning package that combines Latino flair, a subtropical backdrop and retro style.

Most of the hotels along the South Beach streets were once cheap hotels put up during the Depression for working-class holidaymakers from New York. The developers had no money for size or rich decoration, resulting in an abundance of small hotels that rarely rise above three storeys. Architects drew inspiration from the aerodynamic design of planes, trains and automobiles, detailing their buildings with banding or racing stripes, cantilevered window shades and rounded corners admired by aficionados of the Art Deco style. But over a 40-year period, the hotels became low-rent housing filled with pensioners, until the Miami Design Preservation League, formed in 1976, determined to renovate the hotels. Miami Beach's transformation began, and from its once shabby state, South Beach developed an aura of chic.

The area has more than 800 examples of Art Deco, Streamline Moderne and Spanish Mediterranean Revival styles. The annual Art Deco weekend in the second week of January attracts half a million Deco fans from all over the world. While many of the Deco buildings have been preserved, or are in the process of restoration, some are not. One block back from the famed beachfront promenade are some that are a more sorry than pleasing sight. One is the Clinton Hotel, with a cracked façade and peeling paint. Its down-trodden appearance is shared by several of its neighbors. However, the majority proudly parade in brightly painted colors in a role reversal that is a great American comeback.

Lobby with Deco chairs

Bedroom of Room 302, overlooking the beach

The nightlife and the neons, the sweltering heat, the sun worshippers and the salsa – **it's a heady mix**. The urge to dance and be bronzed is hard to resist.

The cost of renovation has been in the millions, but the payback has been much greater. Now no Art Deco period hotel can be torn down without approval, and if one is demolished, it must be rebuilt in keeping with the surrounding architecture.

There are other attractions too, including the mansion that belonged to fashion designer Gianni Versace, which is visited by tourist ghouls keen to photograph the steps on which he was shot dead.

Miami, and its communities like South Beach, is the promised land for immigrants, the recently displaced and the recently retired, all seeking a better way of life or their time in the sun. Many Cuban exiles have established a beachhead here, close to their beloved country which itself is slowly becoming a tourist attraction.

A melting pot for many Hispanics, Miami's Little Havana neighborhood emulates the sights, smells and sounds of Cuba. Tobacco stores sell hand-rolled cigars, *botanicas* offer herbal cures, men wearing *guayabera* (brightly patterned) shirts play dominoes; all this activity set to salsa and merengue music. Alluring aromas of Latin cuisine fill the air.

South Beach's attractions extend beyond architecture. The area has become a magnet for celebrities and fun lovers from all over the world, drawn to its cosmopolitan atmosphere, chic restaurants, pulsating clubs and white-sand beaches. Bronzed boys of all ages cruise the length of Ocean Drive in convertible cars with boom boxes thumping out music at full volume. Taut, tanned and terrific bodies lie on the beach, stroll or rollerblade along the streets. Regular thunderstorms on summer afternoons and early evenings seem to fit the predominantly Latino temperament of the place – flashes of lightning match the flashes of neon, often providing a double light show.

Colorful and amusing lifeguard stations are dotted along the beach, an architectural whimsy with appropriately hot color schemes.

The feverish South Beach energy levels are at full pitch at night. All along the beachfront, it's party time. Competing Latino bands play on every terrace, crowds promenade in the hot night air or sit at the many sidewalk cafes watching the constant parade of tourists and residents going by: the rollerbladers, models, wannabees, hunks ... To help you stay awake and not miss what's going on, drink the strong black, sweet coffee, café Cubano.

The Cardozo Hotel
Miami
United States

Tel: (305) 535-6500
Fax: (305) 532-3563
Internet: www.cardozohotel.com

Diner in Deco style

New York skyline by day

The portal of Grand Central Station

Megaportal

New York City, United States

Grand Central Station is one of the most famous entry points to the city of New York. This old style portal is the doorway to Manhattan for thousands who cross its concourse every day. Off to work, their heads down, few probably glance up at the heroic vaulted ceiling painted with constellations of the Zodiac.

The station's original turn-of-the-century splendor has been restored to better reflect its name.

To many, New York is the ultimate urban destination, the consummate city, home of skyscrapers and towers, night and day adrenalin, corporate success or failure, stardom or anonymity. Thousands of newcomers still arrive here with stars in their eyes, and as the song says, "if you can make it there you can make it anywhere."

One of Manhattan's older downtown neighborhoods is SoHo, once the center of the city's iron and steel manufacturing industry. The cast-iron buildings with huge windows and strong structures capable of supporting heavy loads were taken over by artists who set up loft studios here. They were followed by art galleries, restaurants and bars. Then the big-name retailers started to move in. Now SoHo's concentration of stores draws foreign tourists and local shoppers away from uptown's crowded streets.

The latest arrival on the block is the (Mercer) Hotel. Contradicting its desire for discretion, a delayed opening, the interior design and its celebrity guests have attracted attention and coverage. The hotel has achieved instant popularity in spite of itself. All the print material from stationery to matchboxes has the Mercer's name in parentheses.

The lobby tea bar and entrance to the Mercer's restaurant, "The Kitchen."

The Mercer Hotel

The Reception

"In small and exclusive hotels that tend to be used by celebrities, you want discretion and protection – from noise, phone calls, being photographed, even the city itself – and parentheses suggest that ... " said the graphic designer Tibor Kalman. The theme continues on the bedroom doors, where the number is bracketed.

The Mercer building, constructed in 1890 for John Jacob Astor II, is detailed with Romanesque arched windows, cast-iron columns, vaulting and gargoyles. Its owner, André Balazs, who also owns the legendary Hollywood hotel Château Marmont and the Sunset Beach Hotel on Shelter Island, didn't want something "painfully stylish" for the new interiors. His vision was to provide an atmosphere of domestic bliss (one that you often have to leave home to achieve!). The much talked-about interior is by hot French designer Christian Liaigre, whose starting point was to think of the Mercer as a home, or maybe as a club for friends. "I wanted to make it warm and livable – and calm; to get away from that SoHo people-in-black severity ... that darkness which goes with the assault of New York, the noise, the aggressiveness."

Accordingly, the lobby is more like a living room, with couches and armchairs covered in the Liaigre palette of chocolate, taupe, ivory and lilac. It can seat 100 people, considerably more than the normal living room. Tables and stools are made of luxurious dark African woods like wenge and ipe, a Liaigre trademark. One wall is lined with bookcases, filled with brightly colored volumes on art, fashion and design. So there is plenty to read while having a drink or waiting for friends. There is even a little room behind the bookcase to which you can retreat if you want solitude. This hotel caters to those who like and can afford informal luxury, perhaps the most expensive kind!

The glassed-off vestibule at the front is a bar and entrance to the basement level restaurant, the Mercer Kitchen. Balazs wanted a restaurant like "a big eat-in kitchen, always the place with the warmest feeling and the best conversation," so there are some communal tables as well. The food and service are excellent and not at all of the kind usually found at home!

This casual warm ambience has been meticulously planned. The atmosphere is slightly rarefied, the illusion of peace compared to the traffic noise outside a clever juxtaposition.

The lobby with floor-to-ceiling bookcase

The rooms are serene, a welcome relief from the stress of the streets. Sunlight streams through arched windows, filtered by linen curtains. There is plenty of table space, as Liaigre believes that most hotels don't provide enough space to work or eat at. Generously proportioned full-length mirrors that lean against the wall also satisfy his concern for space. There is also somewhere to hide the shopping bags, with walk in wardrobe storage. SoHo provides ample opportunity for retail therapy, after which you have to lie down on a couch for some time.

The rooms have an air of simplicity rather than minimalism – less zen, more den. These are spaces to relax in as well as relaxing spaces, reflecting the sure yet light hand of this stylish designer. Liaigre believes that the purpose of design is to make you feel comfortable, and his trademark look is livability.

Large bathrooms with enormous showers and marble king-sized bathtubs are based on studies suggesting that this is where most hotel guests spend around 70 percent of their waking time. What they are doing for that amount of time was not revealed.

The Mercer has the aura of a sleek club, at the luxury end of the market in a city where hotel rooms are usually all premium priced. Its atmosphere is that of a super-chic home edged with a touch of attitude, which, for some, will make it even more authentic.

Room (602)

You could be tempted to move in and live here – although you might want to forgo the rubberneckers at the front door on the look-out for the famous. Unless you really are a name of course, in which case this might make it seem even more like home. Here you can wear your sunglasses at all times to avoid being recognized or disappointing the celebrity spotters.

The bathroom of (308)

New York by night

Directly across the street, the SoHo branch of the Guggenheim Museum lacks the distinctive architecture of its uptown parent or its Bilbao sibling. Instead it is cast in the same style as its neighboring buildings, blending in, as the Mercer tries to do.

The hotel's instant popularity and the curiosity that engendered meant that the lobby was open only to guests and their guests. Obvious but tastefully attired security men bracketed each side of the plain black entrance door in the side street. They, not the parentheses, were fending off the voyeurs. Start spreading the news ...

The Mercer
New York
United States

Tel: (212) 966-6060
Fax: (212) 965-3838
E-mail: reservations@mercerhotel.com
Internet: www.mercerhotel.com

Climate Control

There is brilliant weather here 350 days a year, so they say in this oasis town. Warm dry desert air, a landscape of stark rock and lush palm trees, and an all-season, near-perfect climate has made this a favorite and glamorous getaway for years for movie stars, entertainers and retirees – sometimes one and the same.

It is an easy two-hour or so – depending on traffic of course – drive out from Los Angeles, almost in a straight line, just enough distance to travel for a weekend break. In the 30s and 50s when urban sprawl was in its infancy, there would have been more of a sense of driving into the country, and a longer journey from the bright lights of Hollywood. Now, the freeway carries through almost directly to Palm Springs.

As well as its attractive climate and relaxed air, Palm Springs possesses a rich collection of modernist architecture. Buildings designed by some of the most famous names in the modernist firmament make it a Mecca for aficionados of the style. In the 60s, Albert Frey, considered the master, designed the cutting-edge Tramway Gas Station, a low-slung elegant structure for dispensing gas. Now it serves as the Visitor Information Center, and an ideal introduction to one of the town's key features. Stop here for a copy of the Palm Springs Modern map.

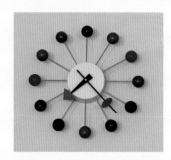

Part of the Rat Pack Suite

The modernist Orbit In has evolved from its beginning as a **classic 50s motel.**

Not on that map, hidden behind gates away from the enquiring eyes of architecture groupies, the modernist Orbit In has evolved from its beginning as a classic 50s motel. It is light years away from that launch date, but still references the past from a design point of view. It has kept the typical L-shaped and one-storey structure of the time, but added elegance and style to the original motel concept.

A house built around a pool is typical of the Californian architectural style, then and now. The temperate climate makes this an outdoor lifestyle for much of the year. Breakfast and pre-dinner drinks are served at and around the pool bar; the water invites a languid dip at any time of the day.

Orbit's rooms are named and themed after and around 50s and 60s architects like Frey, Charles and Ray Eames; furniture designers like Bertoia, Saarinen and Noguchi, and some famous – infamous even – entertainers. The most renowned three, often referred to as the Rat Pack, were Frank Sinatra, Dean Martin and Sammy Davis Jr.

These were crooners with a dark side, rumored to be singing in tune with the Mob. Whatever their real-life story, they were stars in the Hollywood hip set, with glamour and style, as well as talented singers and actors. Palm Springs was a retreat for them too.

There are a myriad of golf courses here, part of the greening of the desert, and of the graying of the inhabitants. Now more retired people live here, and the surrounding satellite towns, than in the 50s when Palm Springs was a party town, a playground of the rich and famous.

Its great weather, accessible location, resorts and the many examples of what were once futuristic home and hotel designs continue to attract new residents and visitors alike. What were the holiday homes of Elvis Presley, Liberace, Bob Hope and other celebrities attract a steady stream of visitors too.

Modernist topiary

Washington Mutual Bank

Orbit in signature

The Bertoia suit

When you are not lounging around the pool, breakfasting at the Boomerang Bar or whipping up a self-catered treat in the amusing retro kitchen – complete with in-period appliances and table settings that some of the rooms have – you might make trips into town on one of the Orbit's cruiser bicycles. You will be pedaling a classic Schwinn, part of a fleet parked in the courtyard ready for guest self-drives. You can bike to buildings designed by Donald Wexler, Richard Neutra, William F. Cody, John Lautner, Raymond Loewy and others, all mapped out and within easy reach from Orbit.

City hall, designed by Albert Frey and partners in 1952

And just off the main street, a tower, the only remnant of a Frank Lloyd Wright designed hotel is undergoing a makeover, another structure that will add to the cache of Desert Modernism when it is restored.

The town center has streets of restaurants to choose from, and some interesting just-on-the-edge-of-town choices. Maybe Norma's for lunch, the colorful restaurant at the dizzily decorated Parker Hotel, or laid-back Hamburger Mary's. Later, try Melvyn's bar, a former Sinatra hangout, for a real trip back into the crooner past.

Back in Orbit, relaxing at your own great example of a Modernist place to stay, you can look up and see, set in the rocky mountain landscape above, another Albert Frey house. Considered an ultra-modern design in the 60s, it is contemporary now.

Nature fans can spend hours, on foot or on horseback, exploring the nearby Indian Canyons, home to the world's largest Californian palm oasis. Fans of the manufactured can tour the forest of wind turbines that marks the approach to Palm Springs, supplying energy to what has become a much-expanded city.

Orbit In is right in the historic "Tennis Club" neighborhood, so those who stay here can play at the club just around the corner. Whether on a court, a green or poolside, this is still a place for serious relaxation, attracting those looking for time out, away from the gravitational pull of work.

Orbit In
Palm Springs, California
United States
Tel: (760) 323-3585
Fax: (760) 323-3599
E-mail: mail@orbitin.com
Internet: www.orbitin.com

Outside the Triton, with the cool Lawrence on door patrol

Off the Square

| The Triton | San Francisco, United States |

The Blue Angels, aerobatic team of the United States Navy had come to town for the weekend. Celebrating Navy Week, the jets put on quite a show and were they attracting attention. The noise was tremendous, and they seemed to be swooping so low over the city that we instinctively ducked as they roared overhead. No strident blue-winged creatures were at the door of the Triton Hotel, but there was a trident, held up by a figure of Triton, the mythical sea deity whose aquamarine torso rises from the water at the entrance. The colorful exterior with its outdoor furniture is eccentric, but the lobby is truly extraordinary.

Even the bench seat looks puzzled, and the carpet is decidedly fishy. The columns are going for gold, the walls are trau-muralized and the Alice in Wonderland Caterpillar's chair appears quizzical. What can it all mean?

The lobby with puzzle-piece ottoman

A corner of the lobby for waiting jesters, with Cinderella's Coach on the table

Its decorative oddness apart, the appeal of this hotel lies in its location, which is just a fortune cookie's throw from the Dragon Gate entrance to Chinatown, and only two blocks from Union Square, San Francisco's smart shopping precinct. (The Triton offers a Shoppers' Anonymous program that begins with a dry martini – sounds good to me.)

Celebrity "designers" have been invited to "do their thing" devising the suites here, from Jerry Garcia of the Grateful Dead to hero guitarist Carlos Santana – who delegated the task to the designer of the band's album covers. Dolphins, whales and seals are given a permanent place in the suite by marine muralist Wyland. For environmentally sensitive guests, there are eco-rooms with ionized air and water filtration, hypoallergenic soaps and lotions, and energy-efficient lighting. "Good-looking, well-behaved pets" are welcome, at an additional charge. Alternatively, if you are not traveling with an animal, the Triton will provide a surrogate: there is a house duck, the Triton mascot, "a shining example of polyurethane waterfowl reproduction" that is a web-footed feature of every room. The Triton duck is a much sought-after trophy. A new duck is hatched every year or so, drawing back past duckhunters to bag one. Next door is the hotel's bistro, Café de la Presse, with racks of newspapers from everywhere, and a stylish dining room – try the confit of duck: disconcertingly, it's a house speciality.

Room 520, with Triton ducks out of water

The Vesuvio café-bar on Jack Kerouac Street, with the TransAmerica Pyramid

The TransAmerica Pyramid building has been described as one of the most instantly recognizable features of the San Francisco skyline, which has a plethora of visual, tactile and edible interests. One of the very best-known sights of this city is its cable car system, pulling the cars and their passengers up what are undoubtedly some of the steepest streets in the world, often with accompanying stunning perpendicular views of the Bay. A tip provided by the visitors' Quickguide, for traveling by cable car – "if you miss your stop, wait for the next" – is practical advice that can in fact be extended to cover much of life. It's a little-known fact that the song *I Left My Heart in San Francisco* is actually a traditional roadsong for travelers – the ones who always leave something behind.

The Triton
San Francisco
United States
Tel: (415) 394-0500
Fax: (415) 433-6611
Internet: www.hoteltriton.com